GRAPHIC STANDARDS DETAILS

GRAPHIC STANDARDS DETAILS

OPENINGS

Wendy Talarico, Editor-in-Chief
Smith Maran Architects, Graphics Editor

WILEY

John Wiley & Sons, Inc.

This book is printed on acid-free paper. ∞

Library of Congress Cataloging-in-Publication Data:
Graphic standards details—openings / Wendy Talarico, editor-in-chief ; Ira Smith, graphics editor.
   p. cm.
   Includes index.
   ISBN 0-471-46530-5 (cloth)
   1. Windows—Drawings—Standards. 2. Doors—Drawings—Standards. 3. Architectural drawing—Standards. I. Title: Openings.
II. Talarico, Wendy.

   TH2261.G73 2005
   721'.82'0222—dc22

                                                                                                2004031047

Printed in Mexico

10 9 8 7 6 5 4 3 2 1

CONTENTS

FOREWORD

Entrances can invoke the wonder that lies behind them. They penetrate the veil between the promises made by the outside of a building and the mysteries that lie within.

Think of the entrance to The Metropolitan Museum of Art in New York City—at street level you look up rows of steps to the front doors hidden by massive columns some 20 feet above. When I first went through those doors, the museum greeted me with the armor exhibit in what is now the reception hall—exciting to see for a young boy. At that age, it seemed that the grander the entrance, the more wondrous the things inside would be.

Historically, entrances were designed with great care and a sense of theater. In Colonial America, for example, the doorway had some carefully thought-out detailing—an elaborate frieze or hand-hewn pillars—even if the building was only a crude box. The ubiquitous beaux arts buildings of the first decades of the last century certainly gave us the grandest entrances ever on schools, courthouses, banks, and city halls.

Then, during the twentieth century, as the use of glass increased and buildings became transparent, doorways often became part of a wall. It seems that only by the century's end did doorways regain prominence—with delicate canopies or elaborate vestibules, and with a new concern for accessibility.

The entrances presented by *Graphic Standards Details: Openings* offer many ways to reconsider how to design them. Instead of climbing steps to gain entry, the doorway can be at street level so that you walk right through and keep going. This is inviting and wonderful for those who have difficulty with steps.

But I also like the book's Hilltop Studio in Pasadena, California, where you walk down a series of low-rise concrete pads to sliding doors. The entry provides a majestic view through the lower level of the house and to the gardens beyond. The glass on the opposite wall gives the feeling of being outside with the benefit of being sheltered. I am intrigued by the entrance tunnel to the expansion of the National Civil Rights Museum in Memphis. It adds mystery to the entry experience and to the museum beyond. An entrance can be signaled by something as simple as a gutter carved from a redwood log as in the Pins Sur Mer residence. The log is a sign of what is important to the owner or what to expect inside.

Entrances enrich the experience of buildings. They are passages, yes, but they are also a signal of a structure's importance, use, or function. They are perhaps the architectural equivalent of the cover of a book, the face of a woman, or the opening course of a meal. They hold the promise of what is to come.

Horace Havemeyer III
Publisher, *Metropolis Magazine*

PREFACE

Since it was originally published by Wiley in 1932, *Architectural Graphic Standards* has served, as its title implies, as a repository of standard architectural details. It has also presented the basic facts of the building—foundations, partitions, and the dimensions of the parts and pieces that make up typical buildings.

But typical buildings aren't the norm designed by architects. Where can you look at the details of contemporary architecture? Certainly there are models in the European and Asian press, but American architects have few places where they can look over each other's shoulders. Most of the learning and experimentation in architecture takes place on-site, but very little of that is ever shared or published in enough detail to really understand how these details were designed or constructed.

For *Graphic Standard Details: Openings,* we invited architects to share their best examples of entries and openings—including the kinds of detailed drawings that are instructional yet seldom make it into publications. We chose to start with this topic as a play on the word "opening" to signify the beginning of a new book, but it is also a universal element of any architectural project, offering myriad opportunities for exploration and invention.

This collection is not intended to be a "greatest hits," but rather to showcase the variety of contemporary approaches to architectural design and detailing. Editor-in-Chief Wendy Talarico, along with a talented professional advisory board including Kevin Alter, Nestor Bottino, Vicki Hopper, Kenne Shepherd, and Tim Shea, sifted through dozens of projects.

After several lively days of discussion and many months of following up on leads, the projects herein were selected from a pool of willing participants. From the modest Lucy House in rural Alabama to the polished corporate entryway of The Reuters Building @ 3 Times Square, we sought a range of solutions to a range of programs, budgets, environmental constraints, and artistic visions.

Julie M. Trelstad
Senior Editor

ACKNOWLEDGMENTS

Thank you to all those who submitted projects, whether we were able to use them or not. I know how much effort is involved in pulling together a packet of materials and I'm sorry we couldn't use them all.

I very much appreciate the time and patience given by all those whose projects are used in the book.

Thank you to the advisory board members who gave their time, graciously reviewed the projects we received, and provided good advice as the book evolved. I am indebted to Julie Trelstad for her vision, to Ira Smith and those at SmithMaran Architects for their excellent drawings, to Kevin Alter for the Introduction, and to Horace Havemeyer, publisher of *Metropolis Magazine,* who allowed me use of the magazine's library and who was kind enough to write the Foreword. Thank you also to Robert Ivy and *Architectural Record* for allowing me to use their library and for their support.

Special thanks to Peter and Anna.

Wendy Talarico
Editor-in-Chief

Benjamin Benschneider.

INTRODUCTION

Construction details are a vital part of architecture. Whether rendered invisible or extraordinarily complex, details in many ways determine both the quality and the character of a building. A powerful architectural concept is realized through its physical manifestation, and the way in which its parts come together—its details—either supports or undermines this concept.

Good detailing means exercising the utmost care at the junctions between different materials or different elements of a building. Through details, parts become a whole; joints, abutments, and seams transform individual components into a building. Good buildings combine technical solutions to these connections with architectural finesse.

While much of architectural publishing tends to focus on the inspiring image, *Architectural Graphics Standards* has long been a reference guide to the inner workings of buildings, albeit normative ones. *Graphics Standards Details: Openings* is put forth with the hope of similarly inspiring a closer look, but this time into a world of exceptional buildings. Like an X-ray that shows us what is behind the façade with which we are presented, *Openings* helps the reader understand the parts of 21 outstanding buildings that otherwise remain invisible, but that nonetheless help to determine the respective buildings' character.

Openings are the subject of great architectural interest as well as extraordinary technical difficulty. As a transition between inside and outside, the house and its situation, the institution and the city, or one space to another, building openings play an especially important role. They mitigate climatic, social, and cultural distinctions. They traverse both conceptual and technical realms. First and foremost, openings grant access to and egress from a building's interior. As a consequence, they interrupt the enclosure that provides shelter. They are the exception to the rule and inevitably demand special attention. An otherwise taut enclosure is now susceptible to the penetration of the elements. Water, for example, is invited in alongside the view or the visitor, and the building needs to be designed not to degrade in its presence. Operability, too, is often a technical feat to achieve. Moreover, one's understanding of a building, or of the world outside, is transformed through the frame of a building's openings.

Several themes and their attendant issues regularly arise in the following pages but are addressed in a myriad of ways. Connecting inside to out through an operable wall or great transparency, and celebrating entry through its signification, sculptural presence, or legible character dominate the buildings in this collection—but these issues are addressed in different manners and achieved through different means.

For an architect interested in designing a wall of windows such that it could literally open and move out of the way, this collection demonstrates both the manner and consequence of several different solutions. Olson Sundberg Kundig Allen Architects present a 30-foot-long, 6-ton operable wall of windows in their Chicken Point Cabin that disappears through a fascinating set of purpose-made gears, chains, and governors that in turn expose the manner in which the door operates. Smith-Miller + Hawkinson Architects employ off-the-shelf aircraft hangar technology to open their 48-foot-long operable wall at the Pier 11/Wall Street Ferry Terminal and similarly adapt it toward a more poetic end. In contrast, Marmol Radziner and Associates fabricated their own steel frames for their oversized glass doors in the restoration of Thornton Ladd's 1950 bachelor pad such that they could be more slender than the industry provides, and therefore minimize their physical presence. Similarly, Isay Weinfeld Arquiteto's House Rua Suiça presents four oversized glass doors that slide away with minimal effort and commotion—the simplicity of which being all the more beguiling when one realizes that each panel is almost 20 feet tall.

Perusing the buildings in this collection, the reader will find inspiring ideas and technical solutions to a variety of other kinds of openings. John McAslan + Partners' gate at 12 Sutton Row demonstrates the power of a beautifully composed and wrought gate for introducing an office and retail complex. The Rural Studio Outreach and Sam Mockbee teach us how to make inspiring buildings on a very small budget in The Lucy House, and how one might utilize 72,000 carpet samples as a building element—through stacking them into a wall and holding them in compression with the help of a continuous wooden box beam. Looking further, the 21 buildings presented in the

following pages have much to say about vestibules, gateways, transitions, canopies, doors, and windows—and the reader is invited in for a close look.

Graphic Standards Details: Openings focuses on a defined aspect of building and examines it from a variety of perspectives. The detailed drawings deconstruct the images of finished buildings. Through these drawings, we are able to take away not just inspiration but also an understanding of the thought that went into making the buildings and the problems that were solved in so doing. Pouring over the materials, the reader is introduced to the art of construction and the consequence of detailing.

As architects, we take responsibility for a building only when we design its details as well as its form. To create good buildings, the details need to be an integral part of the whole. But reinventing the wheel with each detail is neither required nor prudent. An architect learns by precedent, but rare is the American publication that gives away the secrets to exceptional effects. In contrast, this collection serves as a touchstone for any architect interested in both designing provocative openings and understanding the steps necessary to build them. It is intended for the reader who loves to know how things work.

Kevin Alter
Principal, AlterStudio, Austin, TX
Associate Dean for Graduate Programs
Sid W. Richardson Centennial Professor
    in Architecture
Associate Director of the Center for American
    Architecture and Design
The University of Texas at Austin

OPERABLE WALLS

Benjamin Benschneider.

Benjamin Benschneider.

There's a certain freedom in a wall that is there and then not there. A boundary exists and then, with a few twists of a wheel, the sliding of a panel, or a push on a rail, it does not. Such mastery of one's environment is an intoxicating theme in architecture.

Hilltop Studio architect **Thornton Ladd's** renovated 1950 residence, is more windows and doors than house. As a young architect, Ladd was eager to experiment, to try out every trick in his head. And the biggest trick at the time was to blur the boundaries between indoors and out. In the hands of **Marmol Radziner and Associates**, the young architect's former bachelor pad is renovated with elegant sliding-glass doors, a grand set of pivot doors, and

Michael Moran.

rice-paper-lined shading devices that glide electronically along perimeter tracks.

Despite their polar-opposite settings, Pier 11/Wall Street Ferry Terminal in New York City and Chicken Point Cabin in rural northern Idaho use oversized pivoting glass doors to let in watery views when they are closed and cooling breezes when they are open. **Smith-Miller + Hawkinson Architects'** busy East River terminal employs a 48-by-12 ¹/₂-foot airplane hangar door—an off-the-shelf product that operates with a small motor and a counterweight. **Olson Sundberg Kundig Allen Architects'** cabin is a country retreat at the edge of a lake. A 6-ton, pivoting window wall that tilts on a 30-foot-long axle opens via a counterweight, gears, and chains.

The rear façade of **Isay Weinfeld's** House Rua Suiça in São Paulo, Brazil, seems to melt away, thanks to four glass bays that slide behind equally sized fixed-glass panels at either end. The owner could merely crack them open a few inches or slide a couple panels partway down the line, but throwing the doors completely open is magical. The living room becomes an expansive terrace while the overlooking master bedroom is a luxurious balcony.

Operable walls require careful design. Tolerances are tight and materials must be chosen with care to avoid warping and wildly differing levels of expansion and contraction. Additionally, while they are magical and often beautiful, operable walls are also costly.

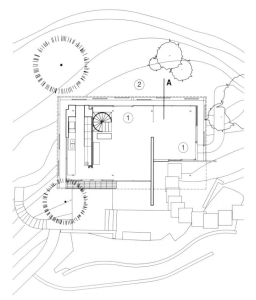

UPPER-LEVEL PLAN

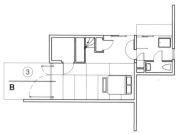

LOWER-LEVEL PLAN

① SLIDING GLASS DOORS
② SHADING DEVICE
③ PIVOT DOORS

Hilltop Studio, Pasadena, California

Marmol Radziner and Associates

A renovated modern jewel opens wide to the Japanese gardens that slope around it.

Marmol Radziner and Associates' holistic approach to architecture was well suited to the renovation of architect Thornton Ladd's 1950 bachelor pad, Hilltop Studio. Marmol Radziner is a 90-person design/build firm with its own metal and cabinet shops, site supers, and laborers. All were employed in stripping the house to its steel frame, restoring it, and fabricating the doors, windows, and light structural pieces used in this 1,200-square-foot house.

Hilltop Studio is more windows and doors than house. There are a few panels of concrete and fixed glazing, but most of the walls consist of sliding glass doors. The frames of these doors are very slender—something that is only possible when they are custom-made. The hardware is also minimal or, whenever possible, hidden. "It's easy to get other doors that are more weatherproof and backed by a large company, but this solution was better aesthetically," says Scott Enge, the in-house fabricator.

To keep direct sun out of the studio, diffuse the light, and create privacy, shading devices were made by sandwiching rice paper between two layers of safety glass. There are two screens on each end of the studio and six on the wide wall. "The idea is to slide them around as needed, not to screen off all of the glass at once," Enge says. "When they are not needed, the screens reduce to a single width on each wall."

The shading devices slide on tracks that line the perimeter of the second floor. Originally, Ladd included canvas-sheathed units that were manually controlled from a catwalk set between the clear-glass sliding doors and the shade panels. For safety reasons (the catwalk is 12 feet in the air in some places and has no railings), the rice-paper shade screens are operated by remote control—a small motor is integrated into the tracks.

The two unequally sized pivot doors in the lower-level entry fill a space that is 7 feet tall and 10 feet wide. The larger of the two doors weighs 700 pounds. The architects couldn't find hinges strong enough to support the weight, so they crafted them in their metal shop. The resulting hinges are of aircraft quality, made of stainless steel with bronze bushing inside so the shaft doesn't contact the stainless steel directly. As a result of this attention to detail, the doors swing open to allow unobstructed views.

Benny Chan.

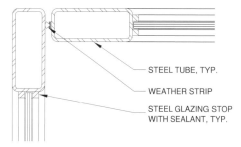

STEEL TUBE, TYP.

WEATHER STRIP

STEEL GLAZING STOP
WITH SEALANT, TYP.

**SLIDING DOOR JAMBS
MEETING AT CORNER**

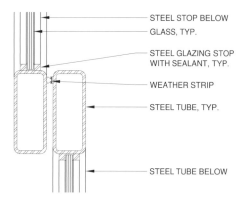

STEEL STOP BELOW

GLASS, TYP.

STEEL GLAZING STOP
WITH SEALANT, TYP.

WEATHER STRIP

STEEL TUBE, TYP.

STEEL TUBE BELOW

SLIDING DOOR JAMBS

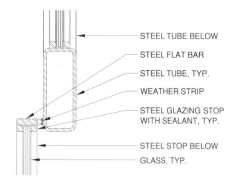

STEEL TUBE BELOW

STEEL FLAT BAR

STEEL TUBE, TYP.

WEATHER STRIP

STEEL GLAZING STOP
WITH SEALANT, TYP.

STEEL STOP BELOW

GLASS, TYP.

**SLIDING DOOR JAMB MEETING
FIXED GLASS PANEL**

SLIDING GLASS DOOR DETAILS

At one corner of the house's second level the sliders
open completely for unobstructed views.

Remote-controlled shading panels run along an outer triple track on the house's
outside perimeter, while sliding glass doors run along an inner track. *Benny Chan.*

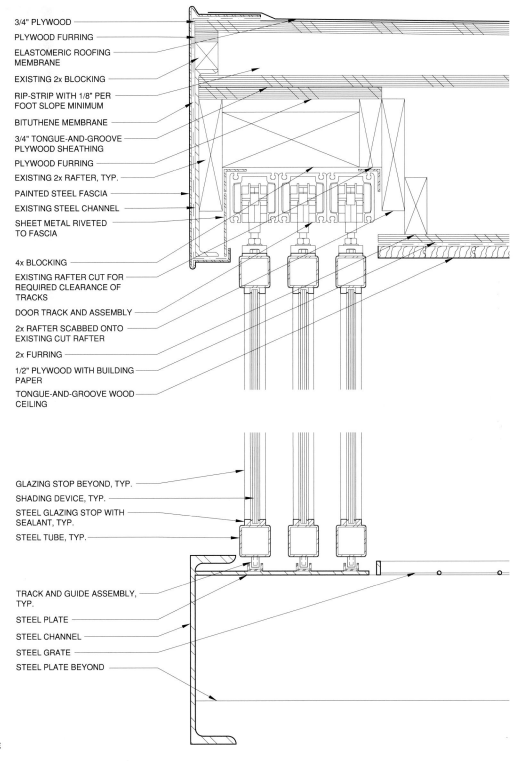

3/4" PLYWOOD

PLYWOOD FURRING

ELASTOMERIC ROOFING
MEMBRANE

EXISTING 2x BLOCKING

RIP-STRIP WITH 1/8" PER
FOOT SLOPE MINIMUM

BITUTHENE MEMBRANE

3/4" TONGUE-AND-GROOVE
PLYWOOD SHEATHING

PLYWOOD FURRING

EXISTING 2x RAFTER, TYP.

PAINTED STEEL FASCIA

EXISTING STEEL CHANNEL

SHEET METAL RIVETED
TO FASCIA

4x BLOCKING

EXISTING RAFTER CUT FOR
REQUIRED CLEARANCE OF
TRACKS

DOOR TRACK AND ASSEMBLY

2x RAFTER SCABBED ONTO
EXISTING CUT RAFTER

2x FURRING

1/2" PLYWOOD WITH BUILDING
PAPER

TONGUE-AND-GROOVE WOOD
CEILING

GLAZING STOP BEYOND, TYP.

SHADING DEVICE, TYP.

STEEL GLAZING STOP WITH
SEALANT, TYP.

STEEL TUBE, TYP.

TRACK AND GUIDE ASSEMBLY,
TYP.

STEEL PLATE

STEEL CHANNEL

STEEL GRATE

STEEL PLATE BEYOND

SECTION A:
SHADING DEVICE

The lower-level entry consists of two pivoting doors, the larger of which weighs 700 pounds. *Benny Chan.*

"At That Time Architecture Was Breaking Out and Opening Up"

Thornton Ladd has closed the architect chapter in his life after 40 years of design work, but Hilltop Studio remains as an exuberant case study in mid-twentieth-century design.

"At that time, the idea of linking the interior with the outside—to the garden—was new, at least in residential work," he says. "We were all working in that direction."

Ladd designed Hilltop while in college and later designed and built a home for his mother on the site. Hilltop was originally studio space, but he soon made it into an apartment for himself. It is richly detailed; as a young architect he was eager to try every design trick in one project. He says: "The whole site is the experiment of a young architect."

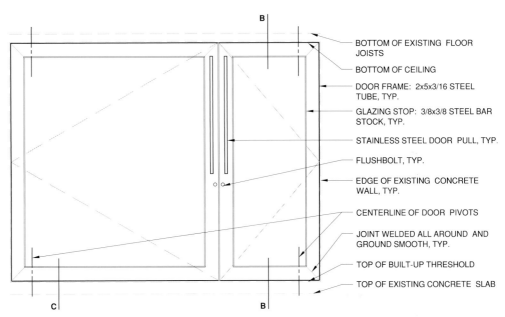

B

BOTTOM OF EXISTING FLOOR
JOISTS

BOTTOM OF CEILING

DOOR FRAME: 2x5x3/16 STEEL
TUBE, TYP.

GLAZING STOP: 3/8x3/8 STEEL BAR
STOCK, TYP.

STAINLESS STEEL DOOR PULL, TYP.

FLUSHBOLT, TYP.

EDGE OF EXISTING CONCRETE
WALL, TYP.

CENTERLINE OF DOOR PIVOTS

JOINT WELDED ALL AROUND AND
GROUND SMOOTH, TYP.

TOP OF BUILT-UP THRESHOLD

TOP OF EXISTING CONCRETE SLAB

C

B

INTERIOR ELEVATION: LOWER-LEVEL DOORS

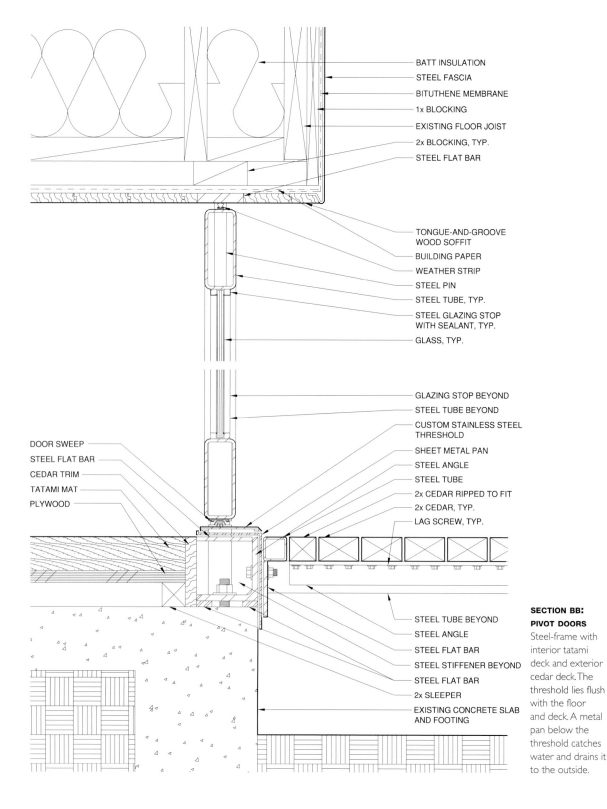

BATT INSULATION

STEEL FASCIA

BITUTHENE MEMBRANE

1x BLOCKING

EXISTING FLOOR JOIST

2x BLOCKING, TYP.

STEEL FLAT BAR

TONGUE-AND-GROOVE WOOD SOFFIT

BUILDING PAPER

WEATHER STRIP

STEEL PIN

STEEL TUBE, TYP.

STEEL GLAZING STOP WITH SEALANT, TYP.

GLASS, TYP.

GLAZING STOP BEYOND

STEEL TUBE BEYOND

CUSTOM STAINLESS STEEL THRESHOLD

SHEET METAL PAN

STEEL ANGLE

STEEL TUBE

2x CEDAR RIPPED TO FIT

2x CEDAR, TYP.

LAG SCREW, TYP.

DOOR SWEEP

STEEL FLAT BAR

CEDAR TRIM

TATAMI MAT

PLYWOOD

STEEL TUBE BEYOND

STEEL ANGLE

STEEL FLAT BAR

STEEL STIFFENER BEYOND

STEEL FLAT BAR

2x SLEEPER

EXISTING CONCRETE SLAB AND FOOTING

SECTION BB: PIVOT DOORS

Steel-frame with interior tatami deck and exterior cedar deck. The threshold lies flush with the floor and deck. A metal pan below the threshold catches water and drains it to the outside.

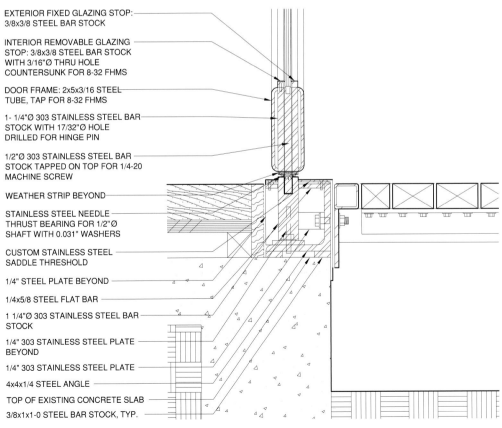

EXTERIOR FIXED GLAZING STOP:
3/8x3/8 STEEL BAR STOCK

INTERIOR REMOVABLE GLAZING
STOP: 3/8x3/8 STEEL BAR STOCK
WITH 3/16"Ø THRU HOLE
COUNTERSUNK FOR 8-32 FHMS

DOOR FRAME: 2x5x3/16 STEEL
TUBE, TAP FOR 8-32 FHMS

1- 1/4"Ø 303 STAINLESS STEEL BAR
STOCK WITH 17/32"Ø HOLE
DRILLED FOR HINGE PIN

1/2"Ø 303 STAINLESS STEEL BAR
STOCK TAPPED ON TOP FOR 1/4-20
MACHINE SCREW

WEATHER STRIP BEYOND

STAINLESS STEEL NEEDLE
THRUST BEARING FOR 1/2"Ø
SHAFT WITH 0.031" WASHERS

CUSTOM STAINLESS STEEL
SADDLE THRESHOLD

1/4" STEEL PLATE BEYOND

1/4x5/8 STEEL FLAT BAR

1 1/4"Ø 303 STAINLESS STEEL BAR
STOCK

1/4" 303 STAINLESS STEEL PLATE
BEYOND

1/4" 303 STAINLESS STEEL PLATE

4x4x1/4 STEEL ANGLE

TOP OF EXISTING CONCRETE SLAB

3/8x1x1-0 STEEL BAR STOCK, TYP.

SECTION C: THRESHOLD AND PIVOT ASSEMBLY

Pier 11/Wall Street Ferry Terminal, New York City, New York

Smith-Miller + Hawkinson Architects

A wall opens at a ferry terminal, allowing easy movement for passengers and admitting river breezes.

Smith-Miller + Hawkinson Architects looked to the air travel industry to find a solution for cooling the Wall Street Ferry Terminal in the summer months and opening up views of the busy East River year-round. The 48-by-12½-foot airplane hangar door makes up a full 20 percent of the building perimeter. Yet it is an off-the-shelf product—a pivot door that operates with a small motor and a counterweight.

The hangar door is provided by the manufacturer as a basic steel framework that can be clad in anything from corrugated metal to an ordinary aluminum curtain wall system—as Smith-Miller + Hawkinson used here. The curtain wall, the same that is used on the rest of the building, is screwed into the tubular steel frame. "These are two ready-mades simply put together," says principal Henry Smith-Miller.

Environmental conditions along the East River are harsh. Winds can be strong and the salt spray is corrosive. The curtain wall shields the door's steel frame and prevents it from rusting. It also provides a tight enclosure. Weather stripping runs along the sides of the door frame, and a flexible bulb gasket at the base keeps the elements out.

In the summer, the open door brings cool breezes into the small building, which, though it is often crowded with people, has no air conditioning. The open door also extends the building's interior space, providing a canopy to shelter people from the sun.

The door's operating mechanism is put on display here. A big cube of concrete suspended from a cable that serves as a counterweight is barely obscured by a corrugated fiberglass enclosure. The door's curved track and pulleys are clearly visible. The movement of the hangar door jibes with all the movement that surrounds this small building and seems as appropriate to the marine industry as it does to aeronautics.

A hangar door rotates inward, opening one wall of the Pier 11 Ferry Terminal. *Michael Moran.*

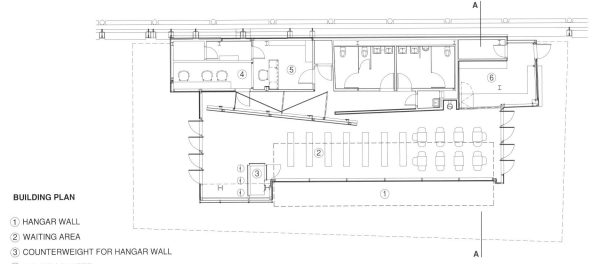

BUILDING PLAN

1. HANGAR WALL
2. WAITING AREA
3. COUNTERWEIGHT FOR HANGAR WALL
4. TICKET COUNTER
5. OFFICE
6. CAFE

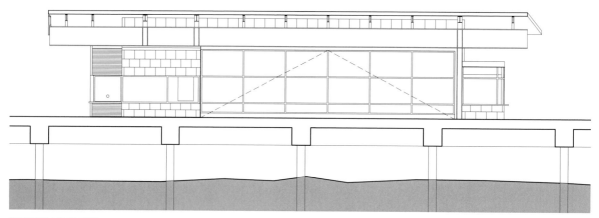

EXTERIOR ELEVATION
The aluminum curtain wall is attached to the steel door frame with machine screws.

The Wall Street Ferry Terminal gets crowded during rush hour. The open door extends the building and opens it to the action on the East River. *Erieta Attali.*

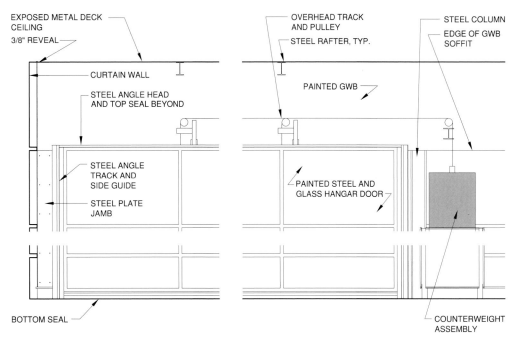

EXPOSED METAL DECK CEILING

3/8" REVEAL

CURTAIN WALL

STEEL ANGLE HEAD AND TOP SEAL BEYOND

STEEL ANGLE TRACK AND SIDE GUIDE

STEEL PLATE JAMB

BOTTOM SEAL

OVERHEAD TRACK AND PULLEY

STEEL RAFTER, TYP.

PAINTED GWB

PAINTED STEEL AND GLASS HANGAR DOOR

STEEL COLUMN

EDGE OF GWB SOFFIT

COUNTERWEIGHT ASSEMBLY

INTERIOR ELEVATION: HANGAR WALL

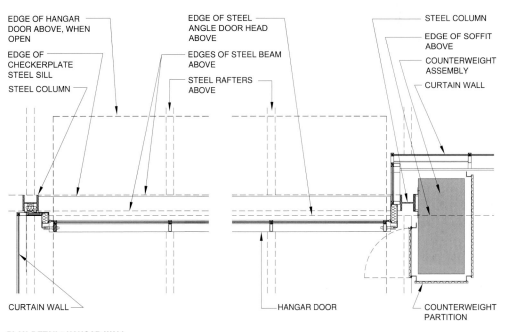

EDGE OF HANGAR DOOR ABOVE, WHEN OPEN

EDGE OF CHECKERPLATE STEEL SILL

STEEL COLUMN

EDGE OF STEEL ANGLE DOOR HEAD ABOVE

EDGES OF STEEL BEAM ABOVE

STEEL RAFTERS ABOVE

STEEL COLUMN

EDGE OF SOFFIT ABOVE

COUNTERWEIGHT ASSEMBLY

CURTAIN WALL

CURTAIN WALL

HANGAR DOOR

COUNTERWEIGHT PARTITION

PLAN DETAIL: HANGAR WALL

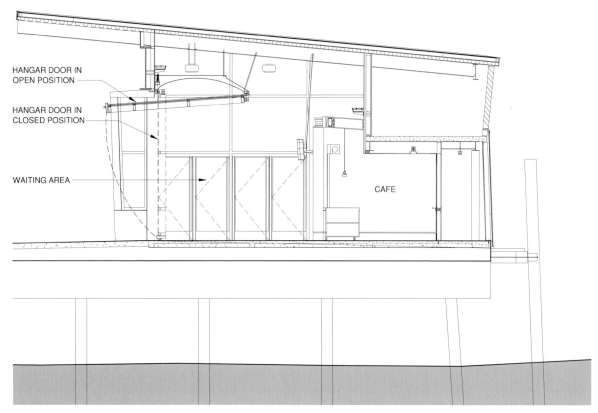

HANGAR DOOR IN
OPEN POSITION

HANGAR DOOR IN
CLOSED POSITION

WAITING AREA

CAFE

SECTION AA: WAITING AREA AND CAFE

When the offset-center pivot door is open, the inboard side is greater than the outboard side by a 2:1 ratio.

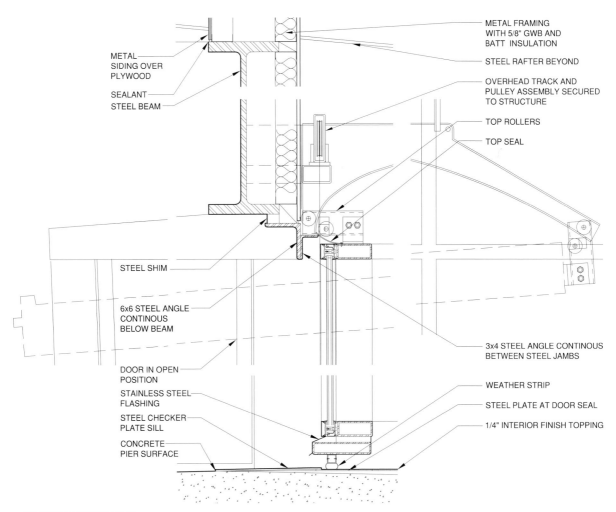

METAL FRAMING WITH 5/8" GWB AND BATT INSULATION

STEEL RAFTER BEYOND

METAL SIDING OVER PLYWOOD

SEALANT

STEEL BEAM

OVERHEAD TRACK AND PULLEY ASSEMBLY SECURED TO STRUCTURE

TOP ROLLERS

TOP SEAL

STEEL SHIM

6x6 STEEL ANGLE CONTINOUS BELOW BEAM

3x4 STEEL ANGLE CONTINOUS BETWEEN STEEL JAMBS

DOOR IN OPEN POSITION

STAINLESS STEEL FLASHING

STEEL CHECKER PLATE SILL

CONCRETE PIER SURFACE

WEATHER STRIP

STEEL PLATE AT DOOR SEAL

1/4" INTERIOR FINISH TOPPING

ENLARGED SECTION DETAIL

Stainless steel flashing protects the base of the door. The bulb gasket at the base, along with a broad roofline, negated the need for a threshold. Interior flooring is concrete with plasticized finish.

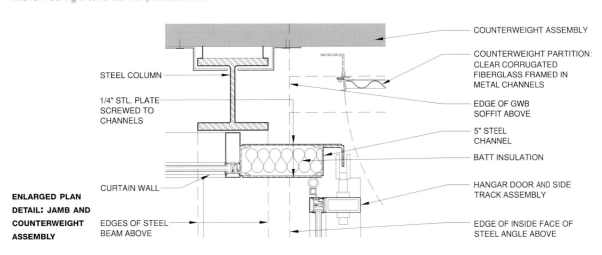

COUNTERWEIGHT ASSEMBLY

COUNTERWEIGHT PARTITION: CLEAR CORRUGATED FIBERGLASS FRAMED IN METAL CHANNELS

STEEL COLUMN

1/4" STL. PLATE SCREWED TO CHANNELS

EDGE OF GWB SOFFIT ABOVE

5" STEEL CHANNEL

BATT INSULATION

CURTAIN WALL

HANGAR DOOR AND SIDE TRACK ASSEMBLY

ENLARGED PLAN DETAIL: JAMB AND COUNTERWEIGHT ASSEMBLY

EDGES OF STEEL BEAM ABOVE

EDGE OF INSIDE FACE OF STEEL ANGLE ABOVE

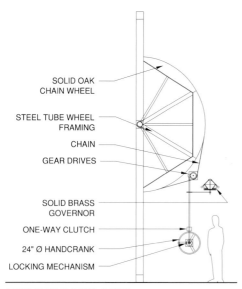

SOLID OAK
CHAIN WHEEL

STEEL TUBE WHEEL
FRAMING

CHAIN

GEAR DRIVES

SOLID BRASS
GOVERNOR

ONE-WAY CLUTCH

24" Ø HANDCRANK

LOCKING MECHANISM

ARCHITECT'S ORIGINAL STUDY

Custom handle for an oversized door. ©*Mark Darley/Esto.*

Chicken Point Cabin, Northern Idaho

Olson Sundberg Kundig Allen Architects

A small cabin boasts two monumental entryways.

Olson Sundberg Kundig Allen Architects added character and functionality to this concrete-block box of a cabin with two king-sized openings. The first is a pivoting window wall that tilts 90 degrees on a 17-foot-long axle, opening the entire living space to the forest and the lake. The second is a purposely disproportionate 19-foot-tall front-entry door.

The 20-by-25-foot window wall, which accounts for two-thirds of the wall facing the water, operates with human-powered mechanics, incorporating a counterweight, gears, and chains—no electricity, no hydraulics. The 6-ton wall pivots on a 1/3:2/3 ratio along a steel axle with ring bearings at either end—similar to the axle assembly in a car. The door is canted inward, making it easier to open and also reducing some of the wind resistance. Bars of steel, which were inserted one at a time into the top of the door, create a built-in counterweight. For safety, a governor slows the door's descent and slot pin devices lock the system in place.

The outer frame of the door is tube-steel; the mullions are flat steel bars. To save energy and keep the cabin comfortable, the wall is made of 1-inch-thick, high-performance insulated glazing. Weather stripping, an important consideration given the harsh setting and the strong winds in this part of Idaho, consists of magnetic compression seals similar to those found on refrigerators. When the owners want less ventilation, they can open a 3-by-5-foot steel awning window that is inset into the wall.

The tall front-entry door is mild steel with reinforced interior webbing to counteract the potential for warpage. It weighs approximately 1,000 pounds and required a scissorlift (and considerable muscle power) to support it during installation.

The custom-made door is set on an angle, skewing toward the cabin's approach from the forest. The door closes directly on the structural frame, which is offset to achieve the angle. The wood-stud wall was furred out to accept the steel door frame. To make the door easy to open, it was installed on a full-length piano hinge. The oversized door handle was custom designed by Steven Rainville, AIA, an architect in Olson Sundberg Kundig Allen's office.

When the cabin's window wall is open, the breezes flow in as they would through an open tent flap. *Benjamin Benschneider.*

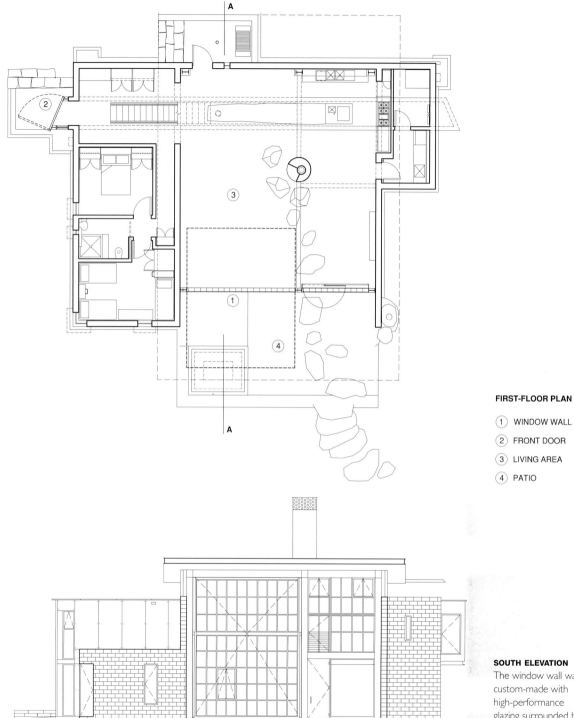

FIRST-FLOOR PLAN

1. WINDOW WALL
2. FRONT DOOR
3. LIVING AREA
4. PATIO

SOUTH ELEVATION
The window wall was custom-made with high-performance glazing surrounded by flat-bar steel mullions and a steel-tube frame.

Benjamin Benschneider.

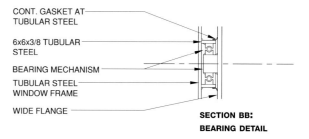

CONT. GASKET AT TUBULAR STEEL

6x6x3/8 TUBULAR STEEL

BEARING MECHANISM

TUBULAR STEEL WINDOW FRAME

WIDE FLANGE

SECTION BB:
BEARING DETAIL

The operating "gizmo" is a sequence of chains, gears, pins, and wheels. The mechanics and the door were custom-made. *Benjamin Benschneider.*

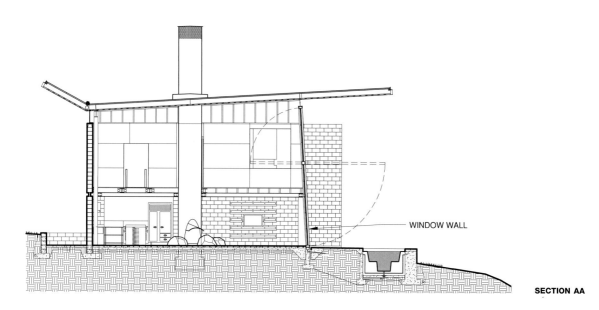

WINDOW WALL

SECTION AA

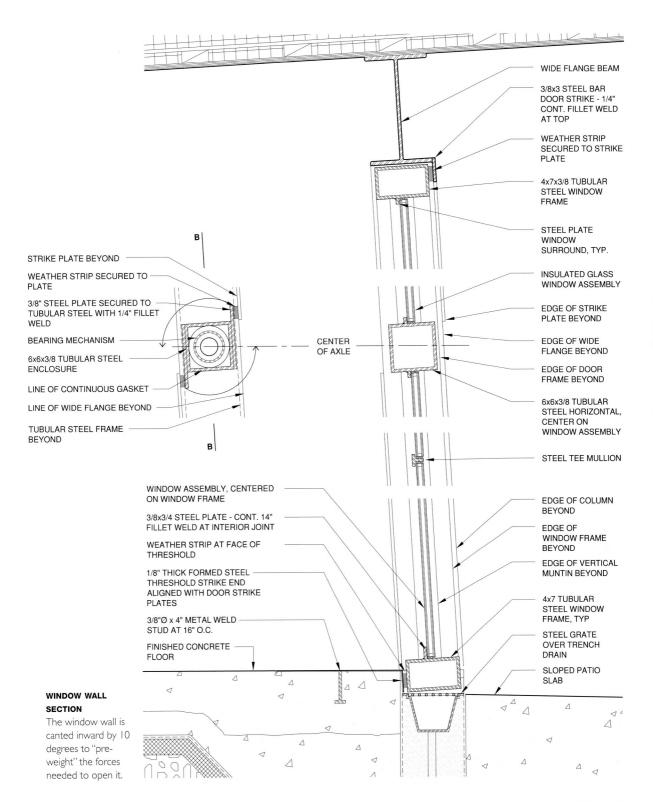

WIDE FLANGE BEAM

3/8x3 STEEL BAR DOOR STRIKE - 1/4" CONT. FILLET WELD AT TOP

WEATHER STRIP SECURED TO STRIKE PLATE

4x7x3/8 TUBULAR STEEL WINDOW FRAME

STEEL PLATE WINDOW SURROUND, TYP.

INSULATED GLASS WINDOW ASSEMBLY

EDGE OF STRIKE PLATE BEYOND

EDGE OF WIDE FLANGE BEYOND

EDGE OF DOOR FRAME BEYOND

6x6x3/8 TUBULAR STEEL HORIZONTAL, CENTER ON WINDOW ASSEMBLY

STEEL TEE MULLION

EDGE OF COLUMN BEYOND

EDGE OF WINDOW FRAME BEYOND

EDGE OF VERTICAL MUNTIN BEYOND

4x7 TUBULAR STEEL WINDOW FRAME, TYP

STEEL GRATE OVER TRENCH DRAIN

SLOPED PATIO SLAB

B

STRIKE PLATE BEYOND

WEATHER STRIP SECURED TO PLATE

3/8" STEEL PLATE SECURED TO TUBULAR STEEL WITH 1/4" FILLET WELD

BEARING MECHANISM

6x6x3/8 TUBULAR STEEL ENCLOSURE

LINE OF CONTINUOUS GASKET

LINE OF WIDE FLANGE BEYOND

TUBULAR STEEL FRAME BEYOND

B

CENTER OF AXLE

WINDOW ASSEMBLY, CENTERED ON WINDOW FRAME

3/8x3/4 STEEL PLATE - CONT. 14" FILLET WELD AT INTERIOR JOINT

WEATHER STRIP AT FACE OF THRESHOLD

1/8" THICK FORMED STEEL THRESHOLD STRIKE END ALIGNED WITH DOOR STRIKE PLATES

3/8"Ø x 4" METAL WELD STUD AT 16" O.C.

FINISHED CONCRETE FLOOR

WINDOW WALL SECTION

The window wall is canted inward by 10 degrees to "pre-weight" the forces needed to open it.

The front door, which is 19-by-3 feet and 2 inches thick, is tall enough to fit the skis through and then some. ©*Mark Darley/Esto.*

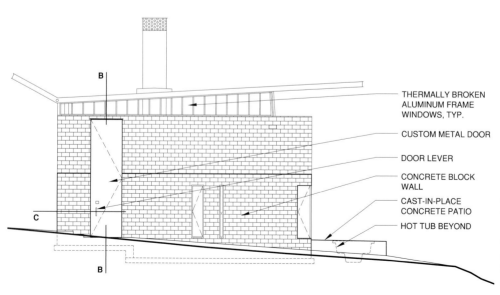

THERMALLY BROKEN ALUMINUM FRAME WINDOWS, TYP.

CUSTOM METAL DOOR

DOOR LEVER

CONCRETE BLOCK WALL

CAST-IN-PLACE CONCRETE PATIO

HOT TUB BEYOND

WEST ELEVATION
The mild steel door is allowed to weather. The framing system is steel with a 2-by-6-inch wood-stud infill.

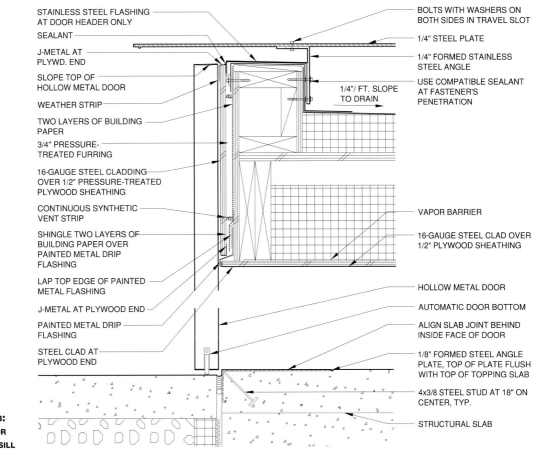

STAINLESS STEEL FLASHING AT DOOR HEADER ONLY

SEALANT

J-METAL AT PLYWD. END

SLOPE TOP OF HOLLOW METAL DOOR

WEATHER STRIP

TWO LAYERS OF BUILDING PAPER

3/4" PRESSURE-TREATED FURRING

16-GAUGE STEEL CLADDING OVER 1/2" PRESSURE-TREATED PLYWOOD SHEATHING

CONTINUOUS SYNTHETIC VENT STRIP

SHINGLE TWO LAYERS OF BUILDING PAPER OVER PAINTED METAL DRIP FLASHING

LAP TOP EDGE OF PAINTED METAL FLASHING

J-METAL AT PLYWOOD END

PAINTED METAL DRIP FLASHING

STEEL CLAD AT PLYWOOD END

BOLTS WITH WASHERS ON BOTH SIDES IN TRAVEL SLOT

1/4" STEEL PLATE

1/4" FORMED STAINLESS STEEL ANGLE

USE COMPATIBLE SEALANT AT FASTENER'S PENETRATION

1/4"/ FT. SLOPE TO DRAIN

VAPOR BARRIER

16-GAUGE STEEL CLAD OVER 1/2" PLYWOOD SHEATHING

HOLLOW METAL DOOR

AUTOMATIC DOOR BOTTOM

ALIGN SLAB JOINT BEHIND INSIDE FACE OF DOOR

1/8" FORMED STEEL ANGLE PLATE, TOP OF PLATE FLUSH WITH TOP OF TOPPING SLAB

4x3/8 STEEL STUD AT 18" ON CENTER, TYP.

STRUCTURAL SLAB

SECTION BB:
FRONT DOOR
HEAD AND SILL

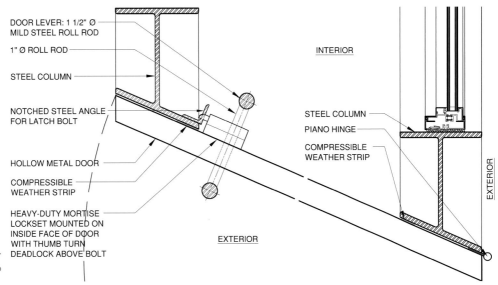

DOOR LEVER: 1 1/2" Ø MILD STEEL ROLL ROD

1" Ø ROLL ROD

STEEL COLUMN

NOTCHED STEEL ANGLE FOR LATCH BOLT

HOLLOW METAL DOOR

COMPRESSIBLE WEATHER STRIP

HEAVY-DUTY MORTISE LOCKSET MOUNTED ON INSIDE FACE OF DOOR WITH THUMB TURN DEADLOCK ABOVE BOLT

INTERIOR

STEEL COLUMN

PIANO HINGE

COMPRESSIBLE WEATHER STRIP

EXTERIOR

EXTERIOR

SECTION C:
JAMB DETAIL
The door is set on a 30-degree angle, pointing toward the entry sequence coming through the forest. The front door has a full-length piano hinge.

Six bays of glass open views to the pool and back gardens. The panels slide open, nesting behind a fixed glass panel at either end. *Romulo Fialdini.*

House Rua Suiça, São Paulo, Brazil

Isay Weinfeld Arquiteto

Oversized sliding glass doors invite views of the patio and pool for open-air living and entertaining.

Isay Weinfeld Arquiteto's Brazilian client wanted a contemporary São Paulo-style house that is transparent and welcoming to his friends, who come often for dinners and parties. While many homeowners prefer to divide a house into public and private zones, the owner of House Rua Suiça asked that the master bedroom be integrated with the living room, the dining area, and other living areas. From this came the idea of a bedroom opening to a large balcony overlooking the living room, the garden, and the swimming pool beyond. The expansive sliding glass doors can be thrown open, inviting fresh air into the house and blurring the line between indoors and out.

Each of the six glass doors stretched across the rear façade measures 6. 41 by 2.55 meters. Including the aluminum framing, the total width of the doors is 14.8 meters. Each door consists of three equally sized sections of 10-millimeter-thick tempered glass. It was not possible to get a single panel tall enough to fill the frame. According to the architect, the glass is dry-jointed for the simple reason that silicone is visible and therefore less attractive.

The panel at each end of the façade is fixed; the sliding doors nest behind. The custom-made metal sliding tracks at the base are recessed into the Roman Travertine marble floor of the living room. The floor continues beyond the opening, forming a deep threshold and a small step down to the exposed-aggregate patio surface. At the top of the doors, the tracks are hidden behind the broad sheet metal box that rims the entire door assembly on the exterior face. This edging shields the entry from moisture. On the interior the tracks are abutted by drywall.

The doors were assembled on-site and hoisted in place with a crane. Yet for all of their weight, they glide lightly on their tracks. Narrow, scoop-shaped handles are recessed in the frame. The doors are the only operable openings in the living area. On cool days, or when there is a strong wind, the doors can be opened slightly to allow just the right amount of ventilation.

The glass panels are tall enough to allow a view to the garden directly from the second-story master bedroom. *Romulo Fialdini.*

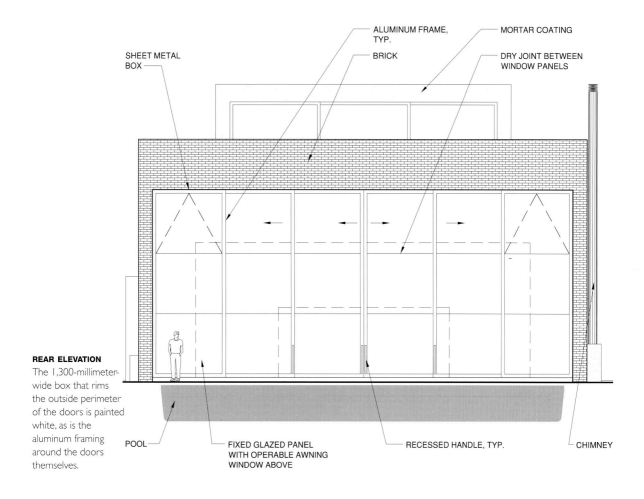

ALUMINUM FRAME, TYP.

MORTAR COATING

BRICK

DRY JOINT BETWEEN WINDOW PANELS

SHEET METAL BOX

REAR ELEVATION
The 1,300-millimeter-wide box that rims the outside perimeter of the doors is painted white, as is the aluminum framing around the doors themselves.

POOL

FIXED GLAZED PANEL WITH OPERABLE AWNING WINDOW ABOVE

RECESSED HANDLE, TYP.

CHIMNEY

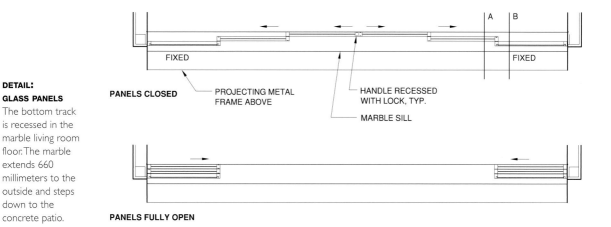

DETAIL:
GLASS PANELS
The bottom track is recessed in the marble living room floor. The marble extends 660 millimeters to the outside and steps down to the concrete patio.

PANELS CLOSED

FIXED

A B

FIXED

PROJECTING METAL FRAME ABOVE

HANDLE RECESSED WITH LOCK, TYP.

MARBLE SILL

PANELS FULLY OPEN

House Rua Suiça, São Paulo, Brazil   29

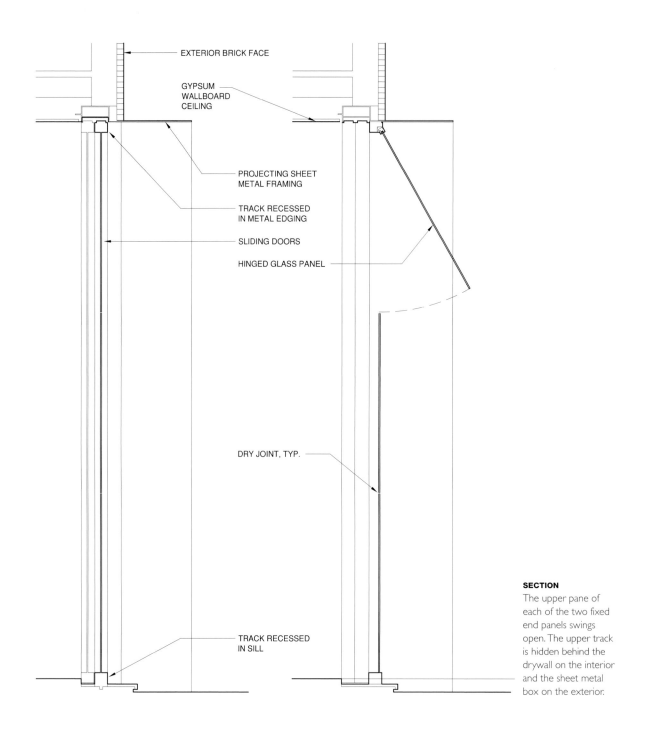

EXTERIOR BRICK FACE

GYPSUM WALLBOARD CEILING

PROJECTING SHEET METAL FRAMING

TRACK RECESSED IN METAL EDGING

SLIDING DOORS

HINGED GLASS PANEL

DRY JOINT, TYP.

TRACK RECESSED IN SILL

SECTION
The upper pane of each of the two fixed end panels swings open. The upper track is hidden behind the drywall on the interior and the sheet metal box on the exterior.

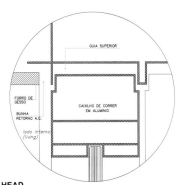

HEAD
TRACK RECESSED IN
CEILING

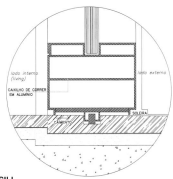

SILL
TRACK RECESSED IN
THRESHOLD

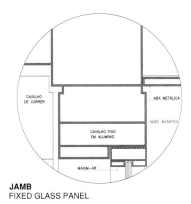

JAMB
FIXED GLASS PANEL

Daytime view of the glass panels in fully open position. *Romulo Fialdini.*

VESTIBULES

A vestibule is a transition space, a zone between street and building that serves practical and philosophical purposes. Structurally, the vestibule may be incorporated into the rest of the building, or it may have its own identity. Regardless, the vestibule is an orienting space where attitudes shift from public to private, from work to home, from wary to safe.

At the Modular VII Chiller Plant on the University of Pennsylvania campus in Philadelphia, designed by **Leers Weinzapfel Associates,** the entire outer ring, encircled by a stainless steel screen, becomes the outer vestibule, though in an unconventional sense. The Chiller Plant is a purely industrial space. The large, simple doors are used by trucks and factory workers. Yet because the faces of the doors—part of the elliptical screen that circumscribes the plant—are a filmy, corrugated perforated stainless steel, they read elegant. The 16-foot-tall screen

Brian Rose.

makes the industrial building into something special—important because of the Chiller Plant's location on a major highway at the gateway to the university.

The entry to the Maurice Villency furnishings store, located on a busy street corner in New York City, must also make a quick impression on passing traffic. **Thanhauser Esterson Kapell Architects** created an angled cube made of alternatingly frosted and clear glass that lures visitors to see the luxurious furnishings inside.

Also in New York, The Reuters Building @ 3 Times Square, designed by **Fox & Fowle Architects**, strives for transparency in the entry lobby. Floor and wall finishes are consistent inside and out, and the revolving doors are all glass with minimal hardware.

Visitors to the West End House Boys and Girls Club, by Leers Weinzapfel Associates, feel the shift from wary to safe when they enter this simple building's two-story vestibule. The streets in this part of Boston hold many hazards for young people. The bright red exterior of the vestibule, a standard curtain wall construction, signals that here is a safe spot, a place where kids can be kids. The steel canopy shields visitors as they enter and proudly identifies the club.

The entry to the Collins Gallery, designed by **Patrick Tighe Architecture**, is a deeply recessed outdoor vestibule—the kind that is only practical in a Southern California climate. The minimal threshold and broad stainless steel and glass entry door work well when there are no howling blizzards to contend with.

©Peter Aaron/Esto.

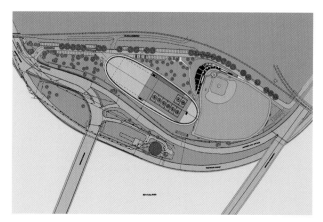

SITE PLAN

Modular VII Chiller Plant, University of Pennsylvania, Philadelphia, Pennsylvania

Leers Weinzapfel Associates

A Chiller Plant becomes a university gateway and offers a study in permeable membranes.

Leers Weinzapfel Associates Architects' stainless steel corrugated wall, which forms a tullelike screen around the University of Pennsylvania's Chiller Plant, also signals an informal welcome to the campus. The building, which glows silver at night, is in a highly visible location along the Schuylkill River and near expressways at the southern edge of the school. It has quickly become a landmark.

The elliptical wall is breached in five locations: Two doorways provide vehicular access, and three more are entry points for plant workers or members of the school's athletic teams seeking access to a sports equipment storage area in the plant. Trucks can enter through the truck doors at one side of the ellipse and drive into the plant via hangar doors (see sidebar "A Different Kind of Garage Door," p. 43) at each end of the building. They may then exit out the other side of the ellipse.

The wall structure is a simple galvanized steel grid. The beams are radiused to achieve the elliptical shape. The sizes of the doors, tucked between sections of the grid, are determined by the dimensions of the grid and the panels affixed to it. The vehicular, or truck, doors, for example, open to a full 17-foot width—the equivalent of six panels. The athletic doors are three panels wide, or approximately 8 feet; all doors are 16 feet tall.

All of these doors are part of the building perimeter and made of the perforated stainless steel screening material bolted to galvanized steel channel. The door frames are also made of steel channel. Stainless steel angles trim both the doors and the openings for a finished look.

The truck doors have a 1/3:2/3 relationship; the narrower door is used by workers for entry to the plant. Many hinges and careful installation make the doors easy to open.

A perforated stainless steel corrugated wall glows at night to create an ethereal landmark out of a utilitarian building. ©Peter Aaron/Esto.

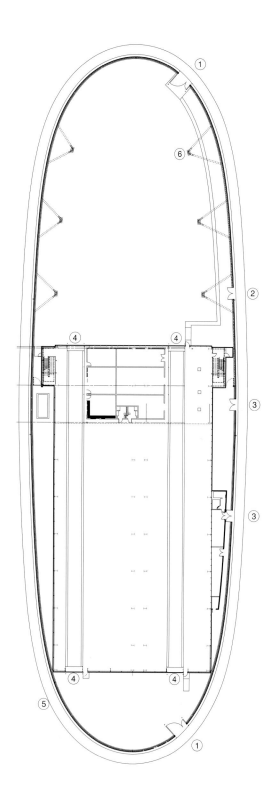

View of the gravel path between the screen wall and the Chiller Plant's glass façade. ©*Peter Aaron/Esto.*

GROUND FLOOR PLAN

1. MAIN ENTRY TRUCK DOOR
2. WORKERS' ENTRY
3. ATHLETIC DOOR
4. BIFOLD GARAGE DOOR
5. TRACK
6. SCREEN WALL BRACING AND FOUNDATION

All five sets of doors are part of the perimeter of the building and made of the same perforated and corrugated stainless steel material as the walls. The door frames and the structure of the doors themselves are galvanized steel channel and are finished with stainless steel angle. ©*Peter Aaron/Esto.*

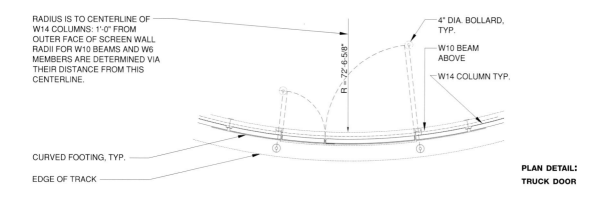

RADIUS IS TO CENTERLINE OF W14 COLUMNS: 1'-0" FROM OUTER FACE OF SCREEN WALL RADII FOR W10 BEAMS AND W6 MEMBERS ARE DETERMINED VIA THEIR DISTANCE FROM THIS CENTERLINE.

4" DIA. BOLLARD, TYP.

W10 BEAM ABOVE

W14 COLUMN TYP.

R = 72'-6-5/8"

CURVED FOOTING, TYP.

EDGE OF TRACK

PLAN DETAIL:
TRUCK DOOR

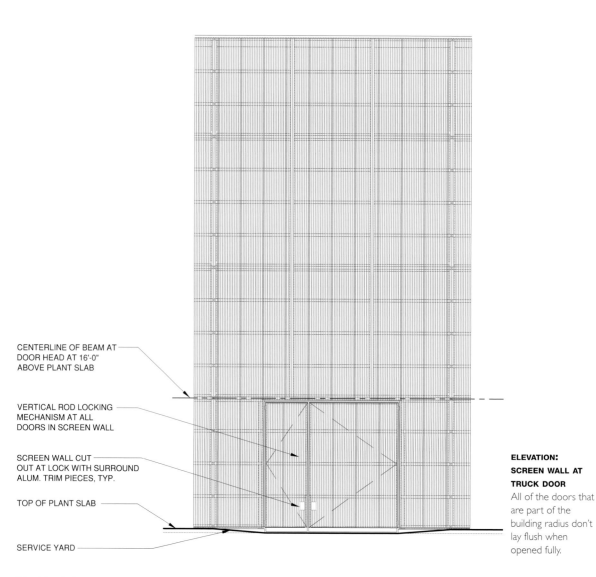

CENTERLINE OF BEAM AT DOOR HEAD AT 16'-0" ABOVE PLANT SLAB

VERTICAL ROD LOCKING MECHANISM AT ALL DOORS IN SCREEN WALL

SCREEN WALL CUT OUT AT LOCK WITH SURROUND ALUM. TRIM PIECES, TYP.

TOP OF PLANT SLAB

SERVICE YARD

ELEVATION:
SCREEN WALL AT
TRUCK DOOR
All of the doors that are part of the building radius don't lay flush when opened fully.

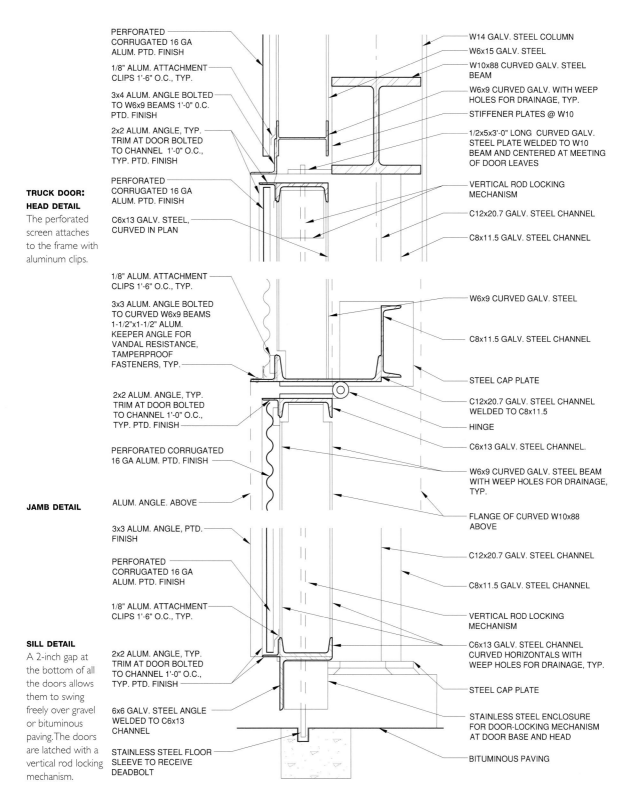

PERFORATED CORRUGATED 16 GA ALUM. PTD. FINISH

1/8" ALUM. ATTACHMENT CLIPS 1'-6" O.C., TYP.

3x4 ALUM. ANGLE BOLTED TO W6x9 BEAMS 1'-0" O.C. PTD. FINISH

2x2 ALUM. ANGLE, TYP. TRIM AT DOOR BOLTED TO CHANNEL 1'-0" O.C., TYP. PTD. FINISH

PERFORATED CORRUGATED 16 GA ALUM. PTD. FINISH

C6x13 GALV. STEEL, CURVED IN PLAN

W14 GALV. STEEL COLUMN

W6x15 GALV. STEEL

W10x88 CURVED GALV. STEEL BEAM

W6x9 CURVED GALV. WITH WEEP HOLES FOR DRAINAGE, TYP.

STIFFENER PLATES @ W10

1/2x5x3'-0" LONG CURVED GALV. STEEL PLATE WELDED TO W10 BEAM AND CENTERED AT MEETING OF DOOR LEAVES

VERTICAL ROD LOCKING MECHANISM

C12x20.7 GALV. STEEL CHANNEL

C8x11.5 GALV. STEEL CHANNEL

TRUCK DOOR: HEAD DETAIL
The perforated screen attaches to the frame with aluminum clips.

1/8" ALUM. ATTACHMENT CLIPS 1'-6" O.C., TYP.

3x3 ALUM. ANGLE BOLTED TO CURVED W6x9 BEAMS 1-1/2"x1-1/2" ALUM. KEEPER ANGLE FOR VANDAL RESISTANCE, TAMPERPROOF FASTENERS, TYP.

2x2 ALUM. ANGLE, TYP. TRIM AT DOOR BOLTED TO CHANNEL 1'-0" O.C., TYP. PTD. FINISH

PERFORATED CORRUGATED 16 GA ALUM. PTD. FINISH

ALUM. ANGLE. ABOVE

W6x9 CURVED GALV. STEEL

C8x11.5 GALV. STEEL CHANNEL

STEEL CAP PLATE

C12x20.7 GALV. STEEL CHANNEL WELDED TO C8x11.5

HINGE

C6x13 GALV. STEEL CHANNEL.

W6x9 CURVED GALV. STEEL BEAM WITH WEEP HOLES FOR DRAINAGE, TYP.

FLANGE OF CURVED W10x88 ABOVE

JAMB DETAIL

3x3 ALUM. ANGLE, PTD. FINISH

PERFORATED CORRUGATED 16 GA ALUM. PTD. FINISH

1/8" ALUM. ATTACHMENT CLIPS 1'-6" O.C., TYP.

2x2 ALUM. ANGLE, TYP. TRIM AT DOOR BOLTED TO CHANNEL 1'-0" O.C., TYP. PTD. FINISH

6x6 GALV. STEEL ANGLE WELDED TO C6x13 CHANNEL

STAINLESS STEEL FLOOR SLEEVE TO RECEIVE DEADBOLT

C12x20.7 GALV. STEEL CHANNEL

C8x11.5 GALV. STEEL CHANNEL

VERTICAL ROD LOCKING MECHANISM

C6x13 GALV. STEEL CHANNEL CURVED HORIZONTALS WITH WEEP HOLES FOR DRAINAGE, TYP.

STEEL CAP PLATE

STAINLESS STEEL ENCLOSURE FOR DOOR-LOCKING MECHANISM AT DOOR BASE AND HEAD

BITUMINOUS PAVING

SILL DETAIL
A 2-inch gap at the bottom of all the doors allows them to swing freely over gravel or bituminous paving. The doors are latched with a vertical rod locking mechanism.

PLAN: ATHLETICS DOOR

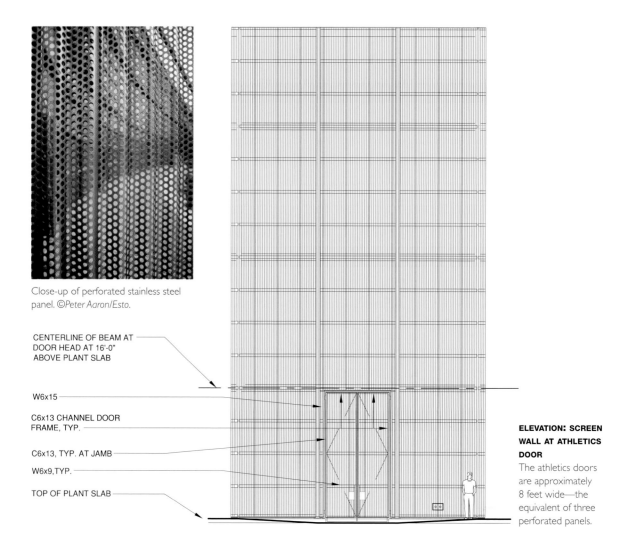

Close-up of perforated stainless steel panel. ©*Peter Aaron/Esto.*

CENTERLINE OF BEAM AT
DOOR HEAD AT 16'-0"
ABOVE PLANT SLAB

W6x15

C6x13 CHANNEL DOOR
FRAME, TYP.

C6x13, TYP. AT JAMB

W6x9, TYP.

TOP OF PLANT SLAB

**ELEVATION: SCREEN
WALL AT ATHLETICS
DOOR**
The athletics doors
are approximately
8 feet wide—the
equivalent of three
perforated panels.

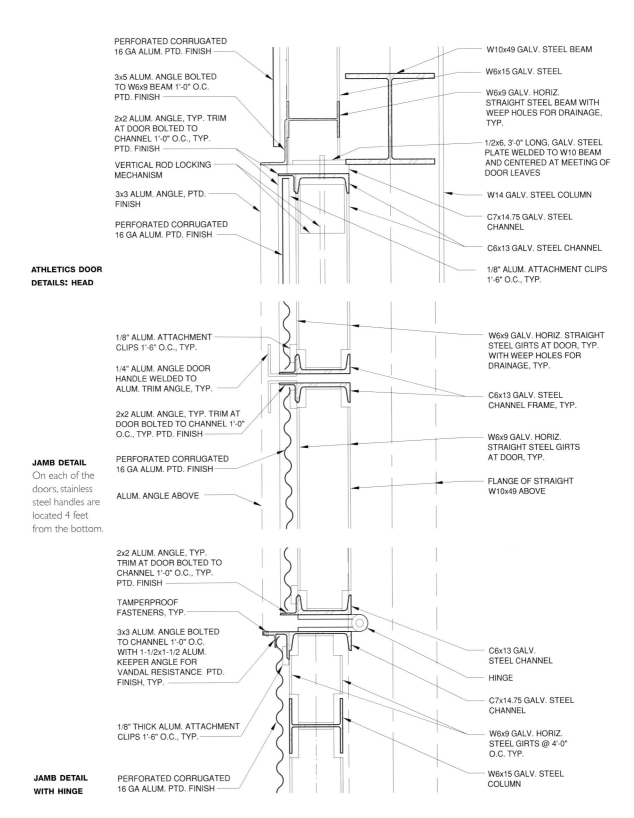

PERFORATED CORRUGATED
16 GA ALUM. PTD. FINISH

3x5 ALUM. ANGLE BOLTED
TO W6x9 BEAM 1'-0" O.C.
PTD. FINISH

2x2 ALUM. ANGLE, TYP. TRIM
AT DOOR BOLTED TO
CHANNEL 1'-0" O.C., TYP.
PTD. FINISH

VERTICAL ROD LOCKING
MECHANISM

3x3 ALUM. ANGLE, PTD.
FINISH

PERFORATED CORRUGATED
16 GA ALUM. PTD. FINISH

W10x49 GALV. STEEL BEAM

W6x15 GALV. STEEL

W6x9 GALV. HORIZ.
STRAIGHT STEEL BEAM WITH
WEEP HOLES FOR DRAINAGE,
TYP.

1/2x6, 3'-0" LONG, GALV. STEEL
PLATE WELDED TO W10 BEAM
AND CENTERED AT MEETING OF
DOOR LEAVES

W14 GALV. STEEL COLUMN

C7x14.75 GALV. STEEL
CHANNEL

C6x13 GALV. STEEL CHANNEL

1/8" ALUM. ATTACHMENT CLIPS
1'-6" O.C., TYP.

ATHLETICS DOOR
DETAILS: HEAD

1/8" ALUM. ATTACHMENT
CLIPS 1'-6" O.C., TYP.

1/4" ALUM. ANGLE DOOR
HANDLE WELDED TO
ALUM. TRIM ANGLE, TYP.

2x2 ALUM. ANGLE, TYP. TRIM AT
DOOR BOLTED TO CHANNEL 1'-0"
O.C., TYP. PTD. FINISH

PERFORATED CORRUGATED
16 GA ALUM. PTD. FINISH

ALUM. ANGLE ABOVE

W6x9 GALV. HORIZ. STRAIGHT
STEEL GIRTS AT DOOR, TYP.
WITH WEEP HOLES FOR
DRAINAGE, TYP.

C6x13 GALV. STEEL
CHANNEL FRAME, TYP.

W6x9 GALV. HORIZ.
STRAIGHT STEEL GIRTS
AT DOOR, TYP.

FLANGE OF STRAIGHT
W10x49 ABOVE

JAMB DETAIL
On each of the
doors, stainless
steel handles are
located 4 feet
from the bottom.

2x2 ALUM. ANGLE, TYP.
TRIM AT DOOR BOLTED TO
CHANNEL 1'-0" O.C., TYP.
PTD. FINISH

TAMPERPROOF
FASTENERS, TYP.

3x3 ALUM. ANGLE BOLTED
TO CHANNEL 1'-0" O.C.
WITH 1-1/2x1-1/2 ALUM.
KEEPER ANGLE FOR
VANDAL RESISTANCE PTD.
FINISH, TYP.

1/8" THICK ALUM. ATTACHMENT
CLIPS 1'-6" O.C., TYP.

PERFORATED CORRUGATED
16 GA ALUM. PTD. FINISH

C6x13 GALV.
STEEL CHANNEL

HINGE

C7x14.75 GALV. STEEL
CHANNEL

W6x9 GALV. HORIZ.
STEEL GIRTS @ 4'-0"
O.C. TYP.

W6x15 GALV. STEEL
COLUMN

JAMB DETAIL
WITH HINGE

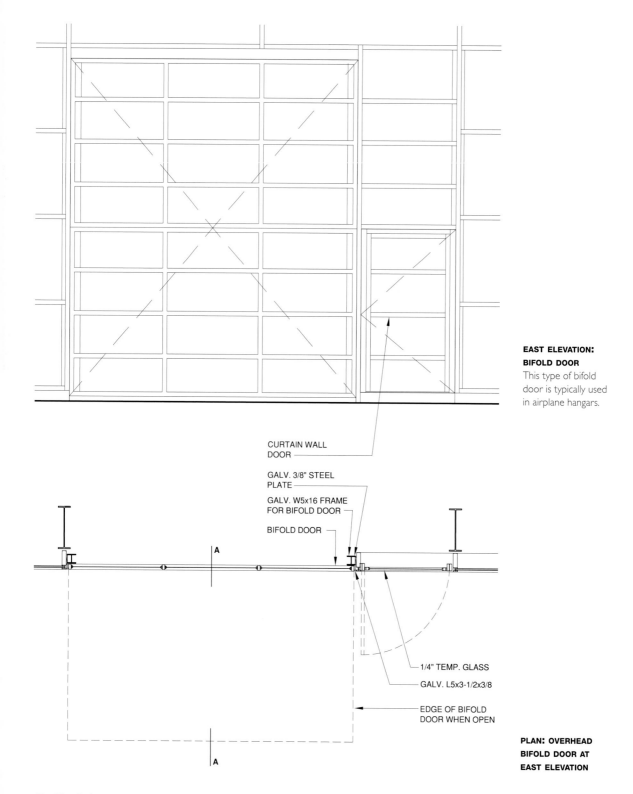

EAST ELEVATION:
BIFOLD DOOR
This type of bifold
door is typically used
in airplane hangars.

CURTAIN WALL
DOOR

GALV. 3/8" STEEL
PLATE

GALV. W5x16 FRAME
FOR BIFOLD DOOR

BIFOLD DOOR

A

A

1/4" TEMP. GLASS

GALV. L5x3-1/2x3/8

EDGE OF BIFOLD
DOOR WHEN OPEN

PLAN: OVERHEAD
BIFOLD DOOR AT
EAST ELEVATION

A Different Kind of Garage Door

Bifold hangar doors are an unusual solution where garage doors are needed. They worked here because the glass doors with a powder-coated aluminum frame fit with the surrounding glazed walls. Also, operating hardware is located on the sides of the door so no track was needed inside the plant. A motor next to the track on one side opens the door by coiling a cable. In its open position, the door forms a canopy over the entry.

The approximately 16-by-14-foot doors consist of two panels. There are 12 panes of glass in each panel. A glass pedestrian entry door, which mimics the glazing patterns on the bifold, is located next to each hangar door.

Bifold garage door in open position. ©Peter Aaron/Esto.

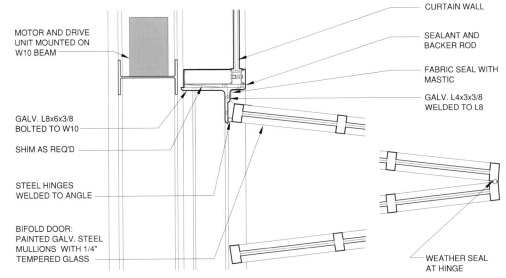

MOTOR AND DRIVE UNIT MOUNTED ON W10 BEAM

CURTAIN WALL

SEALANT AND BACKER ROD

FABRIC SEAL WITH MASTIC

GALV. L4x3x3/8 WELDED TO L8

GALV. L8x6x3/8 BOLTED TO W10

SHIM AS REQ'D

STEEL HINGES WELDED TO ANGLE

DETAIL: HEAD AT OVERHEAD BIFOLD DOOR
The open bifold doors form a canopy over the entry.

BIFOLD DOOR: PAINTED GALV. STEEL MULLIONS WITH 1/4" TEMPERED GLASS

WEATHER SEAL AT HINGE

The cubelike entry creates an antechamber that keeps the weather out and the conditioned air in. *Brian Rose.*

Maurice Villency Flagship Store, New York City, New York

Thanhauser Esterson Kapell Architects

A clear- and frosted-glass cube entices visitors at the Maurice Villency Flagship Store in New York City.

Thanhauser Esterson Kapell Architect's glass entry to the chic Maurice Villency furnishings store plays peek-a-boo with visitors, who catch glimpses of a slender leather chair or a soft woolen couch as they make the transition from street to store.

Located on the corner of a major avenue in Midtown Manhattan, the angled, cubelike vestibule—sculptural, glowing, mysterious—is meant to intrigue and attract visitors. The entry serves a more practical purpose as well: to create an antechamber that keeps the weather out and the conditioned air in. A recessed floor heater tempers the air during the winter. The cocoa-mat floor is durable and slip-proof.

Half-inch, low-iron-content glass was used throughout to prevent tinting and to ensure that the sandblasted portions would be pure white. The complex sandblasting, provided by the manufacturer, features a pattern that bends around corners and carries across the seaming of the glass. The architect selected standard, stainless steel hardware.

Glass fins serve as mullions where the glass is clear. Elsewhere, the mullions are anodized aluminum. The glass ceiling of the cube is suspended from the canopy with two stainless steel cables. These stabilize the glass and prevent movement because of pressure differentials when the door is opened. The rhombus-shaped aluminum composite canopy transitions from ceiling to awning, tying interior to exterior. It is punctured with random lighting—simple cans that look like polka dots. Bluestone flooring follows the line of the canopy.

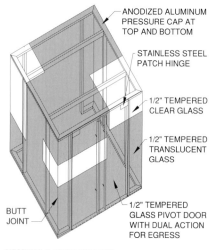

ANODIZED ALUMINUM PRESSURE CAP AT TOP AND BOTTOM

STAINLESS STEEL PATCH HINGE

1/2" TEMPERED CLEAR GLASS

1/2" TEMPERED TRANSLUCENT GLASS

BUTT JOINT

1/2" TEMPERED GLASS PIVOT DOOR WITH DUAL ACTION FOR EGRESS

VESTIBULE AXONOMETRIC

The rhombus-shaped aluminum composite canopy transitions from ceiling to awning, tying interior to exterior. It is dotted with simple, randomly placed can lights. *Brian Rose.*

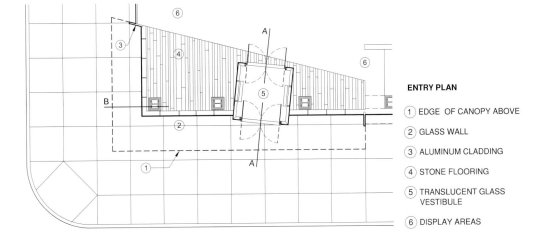

PLAN

ENTRY PLAN

1. EDGE OF CANOPY ABOVE
2. GLASS WALL
3. ALUMINUM CLADDING
4. STONE FLOORING
5. TRANSLUCENT GLASS VESTIBULE
6. DISPLAY AREAS

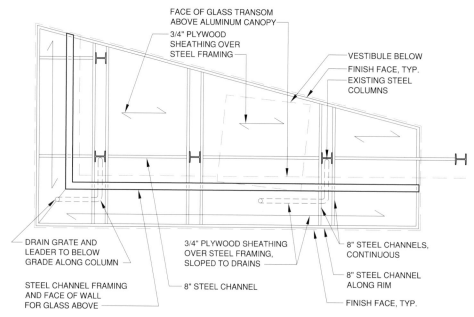

FACE OF GLASS TRANSOM
ABOVE ALUMINUM CANOPY

3/4" PLYWOOD
SHEATHING OVER
STEEL FRAMING

VESTIBULE BELOW

FINISH FACE, TYP.

EXISTING STEEL
COLUMNS

DRAIN GRATE AND
LEADER TO BELOW
GRADE ALONG COLUMN

3/4" PLYWOOD SHEATHING
OVER STEEL FRAMING,
SLOPED TO DRAINS

8" STEEL CHANNELS,
CONTINUOUS

8" STEEL CHANNEL
ALONG RIM

STEEL CHANNEL FRAMING
AND FACE OF WALL
FOR GLASS ABOVE

8" STEEL CHANNEL

FINISH FACE, TYP.

FRAMING PLAN

Brian Rose.

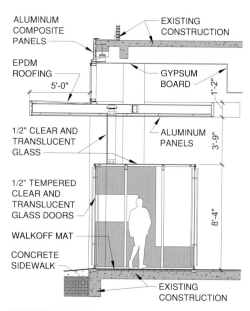

ALUMINUM
COMPOSITE
PANELS

EXISTING
CONSTRUCTION

EPDM
ROOFING

5'-0"

GYPSUM
BOARD

1'-2"

1/2" CLEAR AND
TRANSLUCENT
GLASS

ALUMINUM
PANELS

3'-9"

1/2" TEMPERED
CLEAR AND
TRANSLUCENT
GLASS DOORS

WALKOFF MAT

8'-4"

CONCRETE
SIDEWALK

EXISTING
CONSTRUCTION

VESTIBULE SECTION
The vestibule is 8 feet, 4 inches tall and 8 feet,
3½-inches square.

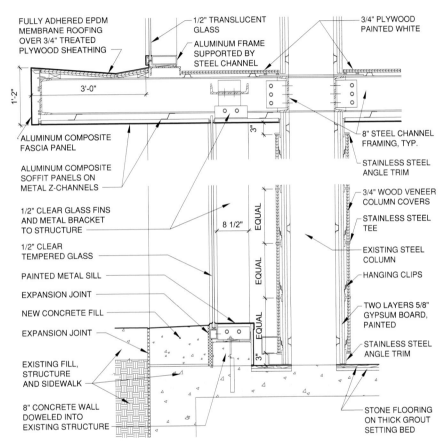

FULLY ADHERED EPDM
MEMBRANE ROOFING
OVER 3/4" TREATED
PLYWOOD SHEATHING

1/2" TRANSLUCENT
GLASS

ALUMINUM FRAME
SUPPORTED BY
STEEL CHANNEL

3/4" PLYWOOD
PAINTED WHITE

1'-2"

3'-0"

3"

ALUMINUM COMPOSITE
FASCIA PANEL

ALUMINUM COMPOSITE
SOFFIT PANELS ON
METAL Z-CHANNELS

1/2" CLEAR GLASS FINS
AND METAL BRACKET
TO STRUCTURE

1/2" CLEAR
TEMPERED GLASS

PAINTED METAL SILL

EXPANSION JOINT

NEW CONCRETE FILL

EXPANSION JOINT

EXISTING FILL,
STRUCTURE
AND SIDEWALK

8" CONCRETE WALL
DOWELED INTO
EXISTING STRUCTURE

8 1/2"

EQUAL

EQUAL

EQUAL

3"

8" STEEL CHANNEL
FRAMING, TYP.

STAINLESS STEEL
ANGLE TRIM

3/4" WOOD VENEER
COLUMN COVERS

STAINLESS STEEL
TEE

EXISTING STEEL
COLUMN

HANGING CLIPS

TWO LAYERS 5/8"
GYPSUM BOARD,
PAINTED

STAINLESS STEEL
ANGLE TRIM

STONE FLOORING
ON THICK GROUT
SETTING BED

WALL SECTION

Glass fins are used as mullions where the glass is clear. Where the glass is frosted, the mullions are 8½-inch-wide anodized aluminum.

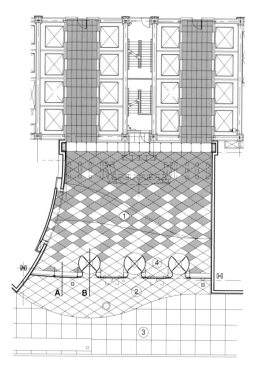

SEVENTH AVENUE

STREET-LEVEL PLAN

1. LOBBY
2. GRANITE PAVERS
3. SIDEWALK
4. STRUCTURAL GLASS
   WALL SYSTEM

The Reuters Building @ 3 Times Square, New York City, New York

Fox & Fowle Architects

The transparent entry to an office building in Times Square features a three-story glass wall and minimal revolving doors.

Fox & Fowle Architects allows the fast-paced ethos of Reuters, a busy news agency, to meet the electric energy of Times Square with this transparent opening. Floor and wall finishes are consistent inside and out while LED signage weaves through, apparently ignoring the building enclosure.

Each day more than 4,000 building occupants move through the mostly glass entry doors while thousands more move past on the city sidewalks. To keep the flow of occupants unimpeded while moving them off the sidewalks, the architects recessed the revolving doors within the building, creating a small alcove or neck. To further augment the flow and for accessibility, swing doors were located between the revolving doors.

The 55-foot-tall structural-glass entrance wall is stabilized by 3-foot-deep, $^3/_4$-inch-thick tempered glass fins. These, along with the $1^3/_8$-inch-thick insulated face glass, slide into 4-inch-deep recessed tracks that brace the glass wall and accommodate floor deflection and movement. While the glass wall resists wind pressure and stabilizes the lateral load, the glass fins hang from the fourth-floor steel structure—which carries the real weight of the assembly.

The weight of the each door is carried by a steel frame, which is also anchored to the floor slab. The door frame is clad with stainless steel. A recessed track at the head and jamb of the door receives the structural glass wall. The all-glass revolving doors with minimal hardware are semi-custom. Graceful S-curved glass pieces form the neck and marry the doors to their frame and to the glass wall.

Reuters lobby interior. ©*David Sundberg/Esto.*

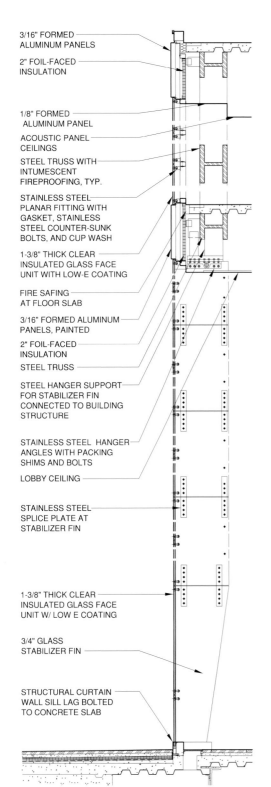

3/16" FORMED ALUMINUM PANELS

2" FOIL-FACED INSULATION

1/8" FORMED ALUMINUM PANEL

ACOUSTIC PANEL CEILINGS

STEEL TRUSS WITH INTUMESCENT FIREPROOFING, TYP.

STAINLESS STEEL PLANAR FITTING WITH GASKET, STAINLESS STEEL COUNTER-SUNK BOLTS, AND CUP WASH

1-3/8" THICK CLEAR INSULATED GLASS FACE UNIT WITH LOW-E COATING

FIRE SAFING AT FLOOR SLAB

3/16" FORMED ALUMINUM PANELS, PAINTED

2" FOIL-FACED INSULATION

STEEL TRUSS

STEEL HANGER SUPPORT FOR STABILIZER FIN CONNECTED TO BUILDING STRUCTURE

STAINLESS STEEL HANGER ANGLES WITH PACKING SHIMS AND BOLTS

LOBBY CEILING

STAINLESS STEEL SPLICE PLATE AT STABILIZER FIN

1-3/8" THICK CLEAR INSULATED GLASS FACE UNIT W/ LOW E COATING

3/4" GLASS STABILIZER FIN

STRUCTURAL CURTAIN WALL SILL LAG BOLTED TO CONCRETE SLAB

Revolving door. *Courtesy Fox & Fowle Architects.*

SECTION A: GLASS WALL

The structural glass wall system is stabilized by glass fins. Both fins and wall hang from the steel structure above and are anchored in a recessed track in the granite floor. Splice plates join sections of the glass fins, while stainless steel fittings hold the glass wall plates.

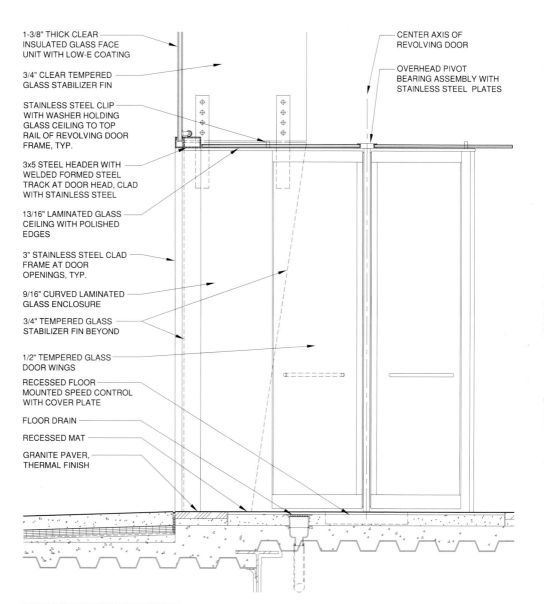

1-3/8" THICK CLEAR INSULATED GLASS FACE UNIT WITH LOW-E COATING

3/4" CLEAR TEMPERED GLASS STABILIZER FIN

STAINLESS STEEL CLIP WITH WASHER HOLDING GLASS CEILING TO TOP RAIL OF REVOLVING DOOR FRAME, TYP.

3x5 STEEL HEADER WITH WELDED FORMED STEEL TRACK AT DOOR HEAD, CLAD WITH STAINLESS STEEL

13/16" LAMINATED GLASS CEILING WITH POLISHED EDGES

3" STAINLESS STEEL CLAD FRAME AT DOOR OPENINGS, TYP.

9/16" CURVED LAMINATED GLASS ENCLOSURE

3/4" TEMPERED GLASS STABILIZER FIN BEYOND

1/2" TEMPERED GLASS DOOR WINGS

RECESSED FLOOR MOUNTED SPEED CONTROL WITH COVER PLATE

FLOOR DRAIN

RECESSED MAT

GRANITE PAVER, THERMAL FINISH

CENTER AXIS OF REVOLVING DOOR

OVERHEAD PIVOT BEARING ASSEMBLY WITH STAINLESS STEEL PLATES

SECTION B: REVOLVING DOOR AND FIN

Curved ⁹/₁₆-inch-thick insulated glass forms a neck and joins the revolving door to the steel door frame and the glass wall/fin assembly beyond. *Courtesy Fox & Fowle Architects.*

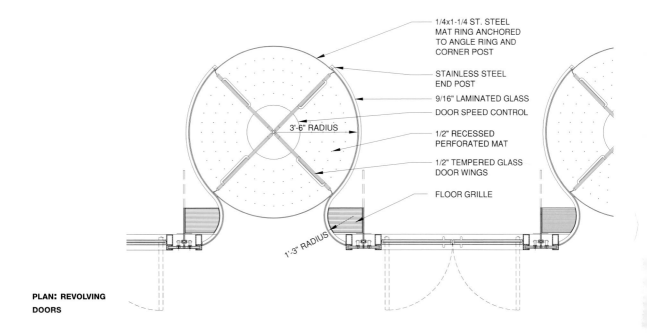

1/4x1-1/4 ST. STEEL MAT RING ANCHORED TO ANGLE RING AND CORNER POST

STAINLESS STEEL END POST

9/16" LAMINATED GLASS

DOOR SPEED CONTROL

1/2" RECESSED PERFORATED MAT

1/2" TEMPERED GLASS DOOR WINGS

FLOOR GRILLE

3'-6" RADIUS

1'-3" RADIUS

PLAN: REVOLVING DOORS

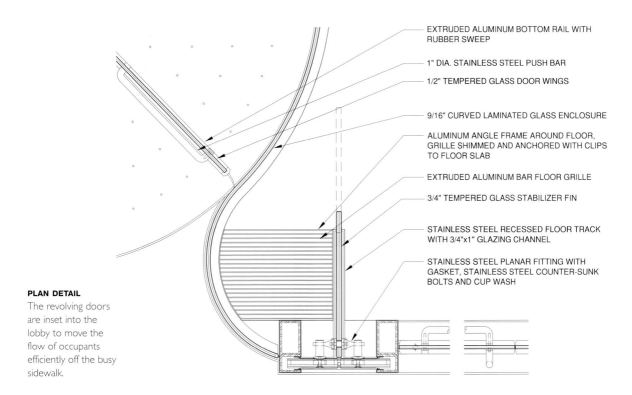

EXTRUDED ALUMINUM BOTTOM RAIL WITH RUBBER SWEEP

1" DIA. STAINLESS STEEL PUSH BAR

1/2" TEMPERED GLASS DOOR WINGS

9/16" CURVED LAMINATED GLASS ENCLOSURE

ALUMINUM ANGLE FRAME AROUND FLOOR, GRILLE SHIMMED AND ANCHORED WITH CLIPS TO FLOOR SLAB

EXTRUDED ALUMINUM BAR FLOOR GRILLE

3/4" TEMPERED GLASS STABILIZER FIN

STAINLESS STEEL RECESSED FLOOR TRACK WITH 3/4"x1" GLAZING CHANNEL

STAINLESS STEEL PLANAR FITTING WITH GASKET, STAINLESS STEEL COUNTER-SUNK BOLTS AND CUP WASH

PLAN DETAIL
The revolving doors are inset into the lobby to move the flow of occupants efficiently off the busy sidewalk.

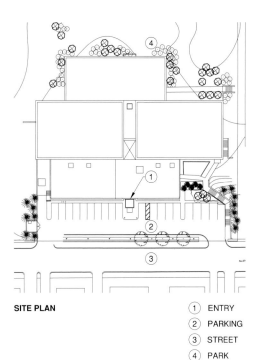

SITE PLAN

1. ENTRY
2. PARKING
3. STREET
4. PARK

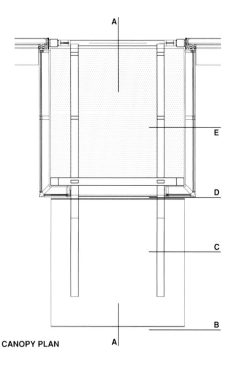

CANOPY PLAN

West End House Boys and Girls Club, Allston, Massachusetts

Leers Weinzapfel Associates

The renovated entry to a Boys and Girls Club signals safety to the children served by the center.

Leers Weinzapfel Associates, when asked to renovate and expand the West End House Boys and Girls Club, was confronted by a dilapidated gray box streaked with green mold and a less-than-ample budget. Located in a neglected neighborhood, the structure could not have been less welcoming to the kids who most need this refuge.

The architect's solution is a new concrete masonry façade accented with a glassy, red boxlike foyer with an unpainted galvanized steel awning that proudly announces the name of the club. The vestibule, which serves as a beacon for the club's young members, is weather-tight, brightly lit, and welcoming to those on this busy street.

The canopy, a single slab of ¼-inch plate steel, extends 8 feet from the face of the building's curtain wall. The tip flips up to form the bottom row of lettering, cut into the slab with lasers. The top row of letters, also cut from ¼-inch steel, was welded in place and is secured with a steel tab. At the other end of the slab, a steel-formed gutter diverts water from the curtain wall. The entire piece is held in place with two 14-by-6-inch galvanized steel beams that tie into the second-floor structure.

Inside the vestibule, a second slab of ¼-inch steel continues at the same angle as the outside piece. It is perforated to let conditioned air from the ducts above permeate the space. The second story of the entry is a conference room alcove. When the canopy is illuminated at night, the lettering casts shadows across the room.

This 9-by-9-foot vestibule is enlivened with bright red aluminum mullions. The galvanized steel letters, which are 8 and 16 inches tall, were laser-cut. *Anton Grassl.*

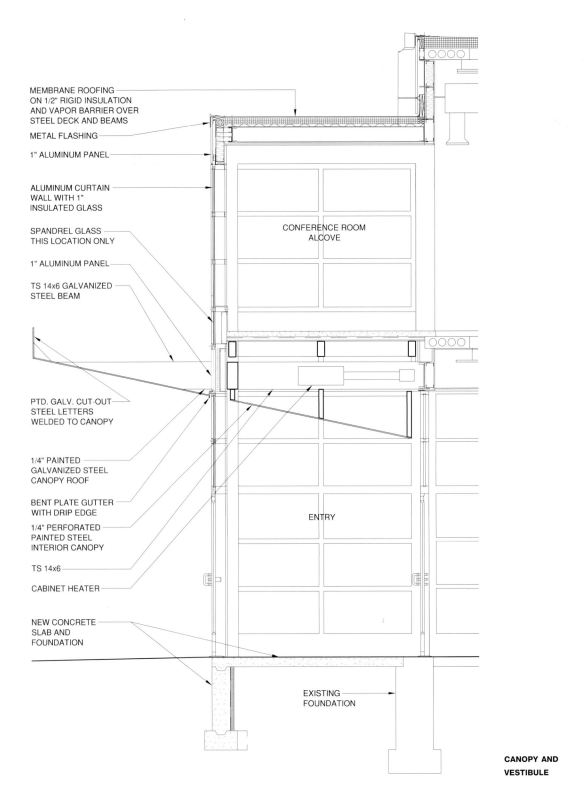

MEMBRANE ROOFING
ON 1/2" RIGID INSULATION
AND VAPOR BARRIER OVER
STEEL DECK AND BEAMS

METAL FLASHING

1" ALUMINUM PANEL

ALUMINUM CURTAIN
WALL WITH 1"
INSULATED GLASS

SPANDREL GLASS
THIS LOCATION ONLY

1" ALUMINUM PANEL

TS 14x6 GALVANIZED
STEEL BEAM

PTD. GALV. CUT-OUT
STEEL LETTERS
WELDED TO CANOPY

1/4" PAINTED
GALVANIZED STEEL
CANOPY ROOF

BENT PLATE GUTTER
WITH DRIP EDGE

1/4" PERFORATED
PAINTED STEEL
INTERIOR CANOPY

TS 14x6

CABINET HEATER

NEW CONCRETE
SLAB AND
FOUNDATION

CONFERENCE ROOM
ALCOVE

ENTRY

EXISTING
FOUNDATION

CANOPY AND
VESTIBULE

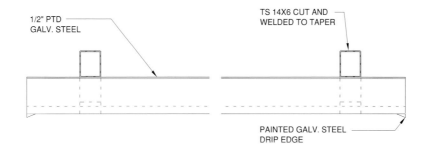

**ELEVATION B:
SIGNAGE PANEL**

1/2" PTD
GALV. STEEL

TS 14X6 CUT AND
WELDED TO TAPER

**SECTION C:
EXTERIOR
STRUCTURE**

PAINTED GALV. STEEL
DRIP EDGE

ALUMINUM
PANEL

ALUMINUM
CURTAIN
WALL SYSTEM

INSULATED
TEMPERED
GLASS TYP.

BACKER ROD AND
SEALANT ALONG
PENETRATING EDGE
AND STEEL TUBE, TYP.

ALUMINUM
CURTAIN
WALL FRAME

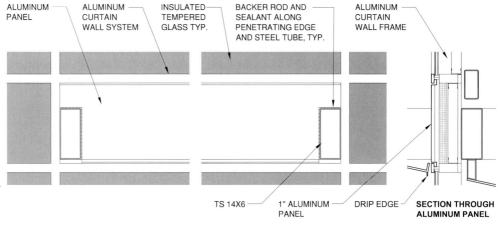

**SECTION D: CANOPY
MEETING CURTAIN
WALL**

TS 14X6

1" ALUMINUM
PANEL

DRIP EDGE

**SECTION THROUGH
ALUMINUM PANEL**

TS 14X6

1/4" PERFORATED
PAINTED GALV. STEEL

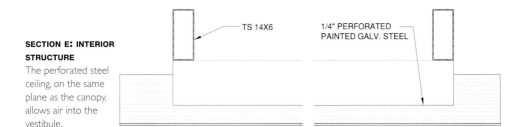

**SECTION E: INTERIOR
STRUCTURE**
The perforated steel
ceiling, on the same
plane as the canopy,
allows air into the
vestibule.

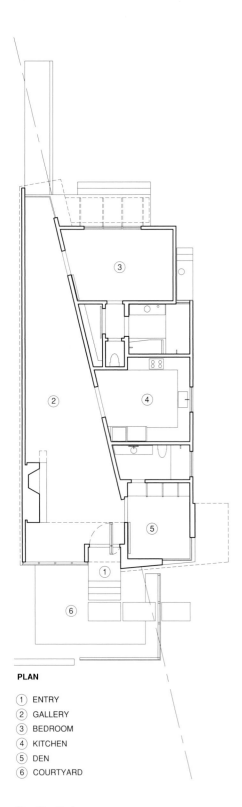

PLAN

1. ENTRY
2. GALLERY
3. BEDROOM
4. KITCHEN
5. DEN
6. COURTYARD

The Collins Gallery, West Hollywood, California

Patrick Tighe Architecture

A single recessed entry serves a public gallery and private living quarters.

Patrick Tighe Architecture used a wide, welcoming entry to satisfy the two very different functions of one small, renovated house. Part residence and part exhibit space, The Collins Gallery needed a door that the owner could slip through with a couple bags of groceries or an exquisite piece of sculpture.

The entryway, which features a stainless steel and glass door below an angled clerestory window provides a visual divide between different exterior materials—the gallery side is an aluminum-frame curtain wall with opaque laminated glazing; the private residence is clad in zinc.

Tighe wanted "a notable entry experience" with the 5-by-9-foot, custom-made door. Mounted on sturdy commercial pivot hinges, the heavy door has a hydraulic opener. Two stainless steel pipes on the interior and exterior run the length of the door and serve as handles. To keep the door clear of clutter, a magnetic lock is located in a box at the top. A card-operated entry allows access when a card is waved in front of a lock device that looks like a doorbell.

The clerestory glass is on the same vertical plane as the door, but it is separated by a steel-plate header. The entire assembly is recessed 42 inches from the façade, creating an exterior alcove. The sides of this are wrapped in zinc. The floor of the alcove is precast concrete planks that were made on-site and placed atop poured concrete steps. The deep recess and a slightly sloped landing minimize the chances of water invading the gallery and allowed minimal detailing. The stainless steel threshold is narrow and almost flush with the interior and the alcove floors. Narrow slots between the zinc siding and precast planks allow water to run off and separate the materials, leaving a cleaner finish.

The ceiling over the alcove holds a nightlight and two roller shades—one for privacy and one to block the sun. These were set above the swing of the door. A stainless steel grate, which hides the rollers from view, is set on hinges so it can be opened to change the lamp or clean the shades. The latter slip through slots in the grate.

The recessed, stainless steel and glass door and the angled clerestory window above it call a truce between the different exterior materials and functions—a gallery, clad in an aluminum-frame curtain wall, glows with opaque laminated glazing, while the private side of the building is clad in zinc. *Art Gray*.

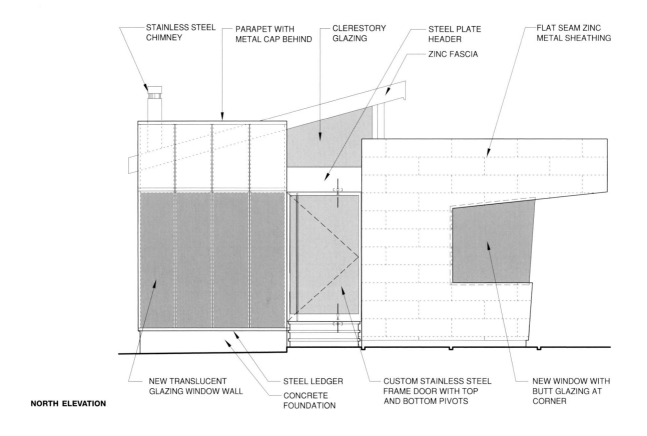

STAINLESS STEEL CHIMNEY

PARAPET WITH METAL CAP BEHIND

CLERESTORY GLAZING

STEEL PLATE HEADER

ZINC FASCIA

FLAT SEAM ZINC METAL SHEATHING

NEW TRANSLUCENT GLAZING WINDOW WALL

STEEL LEDGER

CONCRETE FOUNDATION

CUSTOM STAINLESS STEEL FRAME DOOR WITH TOP AND BOTTOM PIVOTS

NEW WINDOW WITH BUTT GLAZING AT CORNER

NORTH ELEVATION

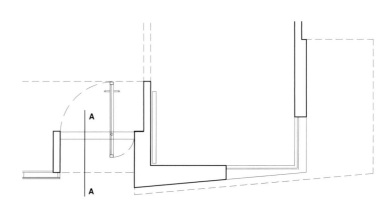

PARTIAL PLAN

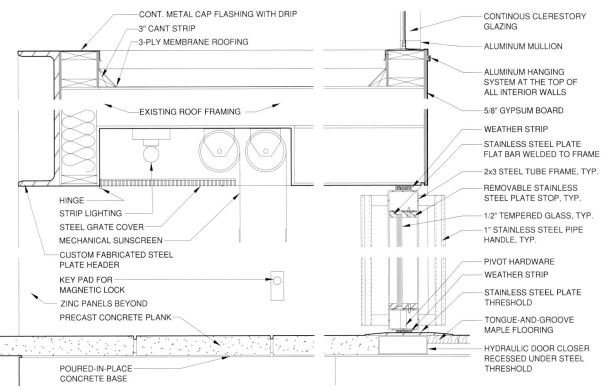

CONT. METAL CAP FLASHING WITH DRIP
3" CANT STRIP
3-PLY MEMBRANE ROOFING

CONTINOUS CLERESTORY GLAZING

ALUMINUM MULLION

ALUMINUM HANGING SYSTEM AT THE TOP OF ALL INTERIOR WALLS

EXISTING ROOF FRAMING

5/8" GYPSUM BOARD

WEATHER STRIP

STAINLESS STEEL PLATE FLAT BAR WELDED TO FRAME

2x3 STEEL TUBE FRAME, TYP.

REMOVABLE STAINLESS STEEL PLATE STOP, TYP.

1/2" TEMPERED GLASS, TYP.

1" STAINLESS STEEL PIPE HANDLE, TYP.

HINGE
STRIP LIGHTING
STEEL GRATE COVER
MECHANICAL SUNSCREEN
CUSTOM FABRICATED STEEL PLATE HEADER
KEY PAD FOR MAGNETIC LOCK
ZINC PANELS BEYOND
PRECAST CONCRETE PLANK

PIVOT HARDWARE
WEATHER STRIP
STAINLESS STEEL PLATE THRESHOLD
TONGUE-AND-GROOVE MAPLE FLOORING
HYDRAULIC DOOR CLOSER RECESSED UNDER STEEL THRESHOLD

POURED-IN-PLACE CONCRETE BASE

SECTION AA: PIVOT DOOR AND ALCOVE

The top of the 9-foot-tall door is flush with the interior ceiling. The inside face of the door is rimmed with a 3/4-inch stainless steel reveal that includes a 1/4-inch door jamb and a 1/2-inch channel. This provides a neat finish for the drywall while maintaining the minimal interior trim work.

Pivot door from the interior. *Art Gray.*

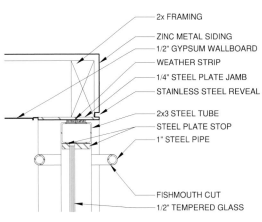

2x FRAMING
ZINC METAL SIDING
1/2" GYPSUM WALLBOARD
WEATHER STRIP
1/4" STEEL PLATE JAMB
STAINLESS STEEL REVEAL
2x3 STEEL TUBE
STEEL PLATE STOP
1" STEEL PIPE
FISHMOUTH CUT
1/2" TEMPERED GLASS

DOOR DETAIL: JAMB

The Collins Gallery, West Hollywood, California   61

GATEWAYS

James McGoon.

Matt Wargo for Venturi, Scott Brown and Associates, Inc.

Graphics announce the gated entry to the Expansion of the National Civil Rights Museum in Memphis, designed by **Ralph Appelbaum Associates**, and to **John McAslan + Partners'** 12 Sutton Row in London. The sliding gate to the Civil Rights Museum is dignified by a quote from Dr. Martin Luther King. The powder-coated steel gate, which rolls on sturdy rubber wheels at its base, is transparent enough to allow an after-hours view of the museum entry tunnel but heavy enough to provide security.

©Albert Vecerka/Esto.

Sutton Row's wood-and-steel gateway is routed to hold stainless steel figures announcing the address. Neon tubes, inserted behind the figures, illuminate the entry.

Jones Studio's Scorpion Residence in Scottsdale, Arizona, includes a 40-foot-long arcade between the guest and main houses that shelters walkers with a glass canopy supported by laser-cut ¼-inch-thick steel plates. The arcade bridges an arroyo, allowing the existing drainage pattern to continue undisturbed.

Venturi, Scott Brown and Associates, Inc., designers of the Trenton Central Fire Headquarters and Museum, have a passion for attention-grabbing environmental graphics. Part architecture, part billboard, the graphics here announce the building's identity and delineate the main entry.

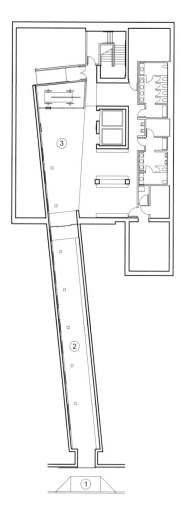

National Civil Rights Museum Expansion Tunnel Entrance Gate, Memphis, Tennessee

Ralph Appelbaum Associates

Dr. Martin Luther King, Jr.'s words add meaning to a gated entry into the Expansion of the National Civil Rights Museum.

Ralph Appelbaum Associates created a concrete tunnel and entry gate for the National Civil Rights Museum when the institution expanded its facility with a 12,800-square-foot building across the street and on the other side of a tall retaining wall. The goal was to connect the two buildings in a meaningful way. The original structure, which became a museum in 1991, is located in the former Lorraine Motel, the site of Dr. King's assassination on April 4, 1968. The museum expansion is located in the Young and Morrow Building, formerly used as a boarding house, and where James Earl Ray allegedly fired his fatal shot at Dr. King.

Due to a significant grade change between the two buildings, the tunnel was necessary to connect the sidewalk across the street from the Lorraine Motel to the basement of the Young and Morrow building. The tunnel is an unconditioned space with exhibits that also serves as the public entrance to the Expansion. The tunnel is closed after hours to secure the exhibits but passersby can still see the backlit exhibits beyond the steel gate. The gate is a quote from Dr. King's Mountaintop Speech, which he delivered in Memphis on the evening before his death.

To keep the gate as light as possible, the letters were made individually and welded into the structure of the gate. All elements are made of ¼-inch steel that is powder-coated to prevent deterioration. The overall thickness of the gate is 2 inches, with the letters recessed about ¼ inch from each face.

The tunnel opening measures approximately 7½ feet square. The 8-by-8-foot gate, set about 2½ inches proud of the concrete retaining wall, rides on heavy-duty, barn-door hardware. Sturdy rubber wheels at the base of the gate glide along a track recessed into the sidewalk. The C-channel is twice the length of the opening so that the gate slides completely open during museum hours. A small metal angle/gutter was added to the top of the wall over the door to prevent dirt from sliding over the wall on rainy days and onto the visitors.

A steel gate, bearing a quotation from Dr. Martin Luther King, Jr.'s Mountaintop Speech, forms the entryway to a tunnel exhibit space and an extension of the National Civil Rights Museum. ©*Albert Vecerka/Esto.*

Exhibits in the original portion of the museum leave off at Dr. King's assassination, while the new museum covers events that have unfolded in the civil and human rights movements since. The tunnel is symbolic of death. It contains a series of light-box displays that depict Dr. King's funeral and a soundscape that plays music from the funeral, while quotations from famous individuals reacting to Dr. King's death are featured on electronic message displays. ©Albert Vecerka/Esto.

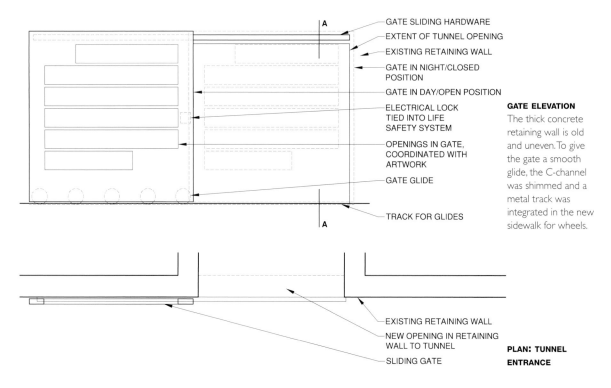

GATE SLIDING HARDWARE
EXTENT OF TUNNEL OPENING
EXISTING RETAINING WALL
GATE IN NIGHT/CLOSED POSITION
GATE IN DAY/OPEN POSITION
ELECTRICAL LOCK TIED INTO LIFE SAFETY SYSTEM
OPENINGS IN GATE, COORDINATED WITH ARTWORK
GATE GLIDE
TRACK FOR GLIDES

GATE ELEVATION
The thick concrete retaining wall is old and uneven. To give the gate a smooth glide, the C-channel was shimmed and a metal track was integrated in the new sidewalk for wheels.

EXISTING RETAINING WALL
NEW OPENING IN RETAINING WALL TO TUNNEL
SLIDING GATE

PLAN: TUNNEL ENTRANCE

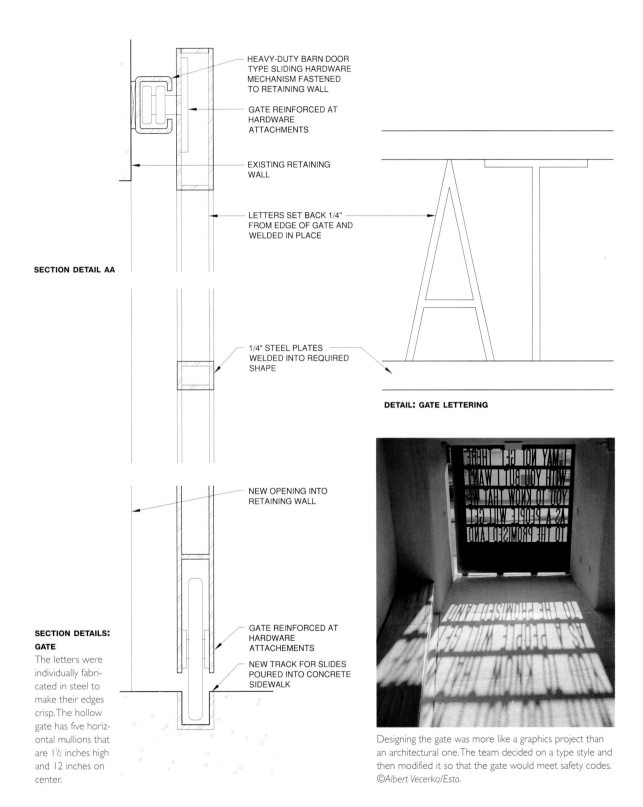

HEAVY-DUTY BARN DOOR TYPE SLIDING HARDWARE MECHANISM FASTENED TO RETAINING WALL

GATE REINFORCED AT HARDWARE ATTACHMENTS

EXISTING RETAINING WALL

LETTERS SET BACK 1/4" FROM EDGE OF GATE AND WELDED IN PLACE

SECTION DETAIL AA

1/4" STEEL PLATES WELDED INTO REQUIRED SHAPE

DETAIL: GATE LETTERING

NEW OPENING INTO RETAINING WALL

GATE REINFORCED AT HARDWARE ATTACHMENTS

NEW TRACK FOR SLIDES POURED INTO CONCRETE SIDEWALK

SECTION DETAILS: GATE

The letters were individually fabricated in steel to make their edges crisp. The hollow gate has five horizontal mullions that are 1½ inches high and 12 inches on center.

Designing the gate was more like a graphics project than an architectural one. The team decided on a type style and then modified it so that the gate would meet safety codes.
©*Albert Vecerka/Esto.*

National Civil Rights Museum Expansion Tunnel Entrance Gate, Memphis, Tennessee   67

Peter Cook.

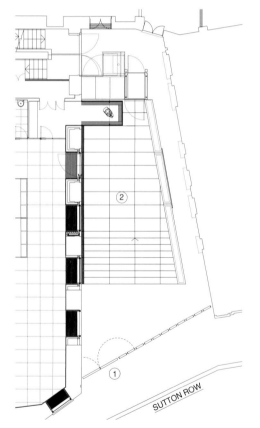

SITE PLAN

① GATE ENTRY

② COURTYARD

12 Sutton Row, London

John McAslan + Partners

At The Courtyard, 12 Sutton Row, in London's Soho, a wood-and-steel gateway signals the entry.

John McAslan + Partners had three challenges in devising an entry to The Courtyard, 12 Sutton Row, an office and retail complex in a group of eighteenth-century buildings. First, security is a concern in this rough-and-ready section of Soho. The entry needed to provide actual as well as visual impermeability, offering only selected views in and out. Second, the client's strict environmental policy governed the selection of materials. Lastly, the entry needed to be bright and bold, signaling the transformed building and clearly announcing the entrance area.

The architect's solution is a substantial wood-and-steel gateway, which leads to a paved courtyard. Entries for the individual buildings front this courtyard, providing a safe and central access point. During business hours, the gate remains one-third open. A manned security pod within the courtyard is, however, clearly visible to passers-by. When the gate is closed in the evenings, those wishing to enter must use a security keypad and a swipe card. A camera is also trained on the entry.

The powder-coated steel used for the gate frame and most of the slats was selected for its strength. Hardwood slats are used exclusively around the lettering and alternate with the steel elsewhere. The wood is routed to hold the stainless steel lettering. Neon tubes, inserted behind the letters, illuminate the entry. The carefully spaced address, designed by the architects, became the logo of the development. The same fonts are used to announce "The Courtyard" in stainless steel lettering on the brick building.

The gate is primarily cantilevered from the ground. It is affixed to the building on the left end; the support post is recessed in the old brick. The remaining steel posts extend 750 millimeters below grade, while the concrete foundations continue for another 750 millimeters. A concrete strip rail supports the gate as it opens. The steel elements of the gate make it heavy. A hydraulic opening device assists users; the device also closes the gate automatically and locks it in position.

A paved courtyard may be glimpsed between the gate's slats. The gate is 3.8 meters tall. *Courtesy James Macauley.*

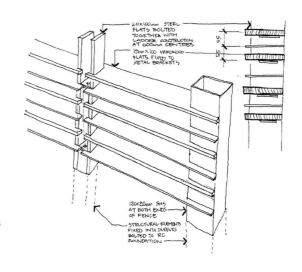

DETAIL: GATEPOSTS
Architect's original
drawings.

Stainless steel letters are inset into sustainably harvested Iroko-wood slats. *Courtesy James Macauley.*

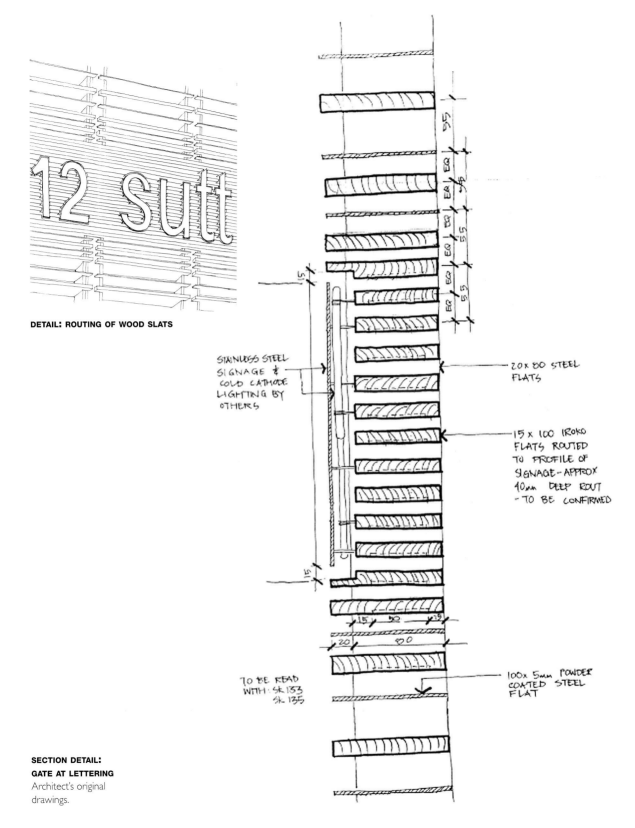

DETAIL: ROUTING OF WOOD SLATS

STAINLESS STEEL
SIGNAGE &
COLD CATHODE
LIGHTING BY
OTHERS

20 x 80 STEEL
FLATS

15 x 100 IROKO
FLATS ROUTED
TO PROFILE OF
SIGNAGE - APPROX
10mm DEEP ROUT
- TO BE CONFIRMED

100 x 5mm POWDER
COATED STEEL
FLAT

TO BE READ
WITH SK 133
SK 135

SECTION DETAIL:
GATE AT LETTERING
Architect's original
drawings.

View from inside the courtyard. *Courtesy John McAslan + Partners.*

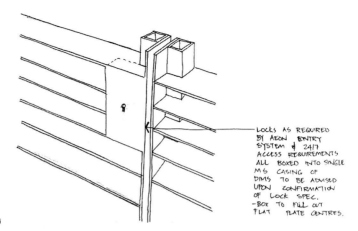

GATE DETAILS: LOCK CASING

LOCKS AS REQUIRED BY AEON ENTRY SYSTEM & 24/7 ACCESS REQUIREMENTS ALL BOXED INTO SINGLE MS CASING OF DIMS TO BE ADVISED UPON CONFIRMATION OF LOCK SPEC.
-BOX TO FILL OUT FLAT PLATE CENTRES.

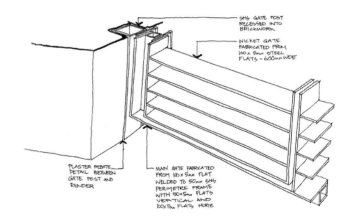

RECESSED POST

The gatepost is recessed into brickwork on one side; however, on the other side it butts against a historic church.

SHS GATE POST RECESSED INTO BRICKWORK

WICKET GATE FABRICATED FROM 100 x 5mm STEEL FLATS - 600mm WIDE

PLASTER REBATE DETAIL BETWEEN GATE POST AND RENDER

MAIN GATE FABRICATED FROM 100 x 5mm FLAT WELDED TO 50mm SHS PERIMETRE FRAME WITH 50x5mm FLATS VERTICAL AND 100x5mm FLATS HORIZ.

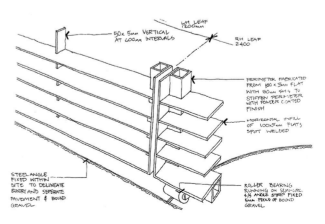

GATE EDGE

The wood slats are affixed to metal brackets for strength and stability.

ARCHITECT'S ORIGINAL DRAWINGS

50 x 5mm VERTICAL AT 600mm INTERVALS

LH LEAF 1200mm

RH LEAF 2400

PERIMETER FABRICATED FROM 100 x 5mm FLAT WITH 50mm SHS TO STIFFEN PERIMETER WITH POWDER COATED FINISH

HORIZONTAL INFILL OF 100x5mm FLATS SPOT WELDED

STEEL ANGLE FIXED WITHIN SITE TO DELINEATE BOUNDRY AND SEPERATE PAVEMENT & BOUND GRAVEL

ROLLER BEARING RUNNING ON SEMI-CIRC. 6/5 ANGLE STRIP FIXED 5mm PROUD OF BOUND GRAVEL

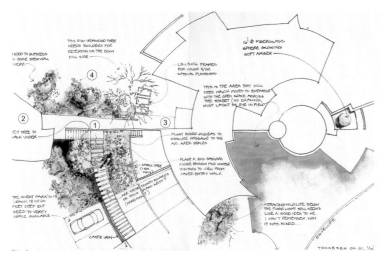

ORIGINAL LANDSCAPE PLAN

(1) ARCADE

(2) GUEST HOUSE

(3) MAIN HOUSE

(4) ARROYO

Scorpion Residence
Scottsdale, Arizona

Jones Studio, Inc.

A carefully orchestrated arcade links the guest and main houses at the Scorpion Residence.

Jones Studio designed a walkway that not only shelters residents and visitors moving between the guesthouse and the main house, it also provides selected views of a nearby canyon and the mountains in the distance.

The 40-foot-long walkway follows an axis that runs from the center point of the circular pool to the edge of the property. The walkway itself is wedge-shaped—at its narrowest point, the path is 4 feet, widening to 6 feet at the guesthouse. It tops a monolithically poured, cast-in-place concrete wall and includes a bridge that spans a deep arroyo running through the property. The bridge allows the existing drainage pattern to continue undisturbed. The high fly-ash-content concrete is pigmented to a shade of purple that matches the soil.

There are stunning mountain views on one side of the arcade, but the architect blocks them with a 7-foot-tall concrete wall—except for a small preview afforded by an 8-by-24-inch slot in the concrete. The dramatic view is saved for the main house. Travelers across the arcade, instead, have their attentions focused on the tumbling boulders of the arroyo, framed by a 42-inch-tall glass balustrade.

The glass canopy is supported by ¼-inch-thick steel plates that are laser-cut into a curvilinear pattern. The brackets are 4 feet tall, but the arms vary in length, growing as the walkway widens. They are fixed to the concrete at two points with steel dowels. The inside vertical edges are held ¼ inch away from the wall, allowing the light to shine through and giving a lighter look.

The canopy has a top layer of ⅛-inch solar-gray glass, a bottom layer of ⅛-inch clear glass (both layers tempered), and a translucent inner layer of laminate.

The balustrade, made of ½-inch tempered glass, is supported by custom-made stainless steel brackets. The glass is pierced in two places by ¼-inch stainless steel studs that lock into 1½-inch stainless steel "buttons." These, together with neoprene washers, grip the glass panels and hold them tight to the edge of the walkway.

James McGoon.

The Scorpion Residence includes a sizeable guest house (left). ©*Mark Borsclair Photography.*

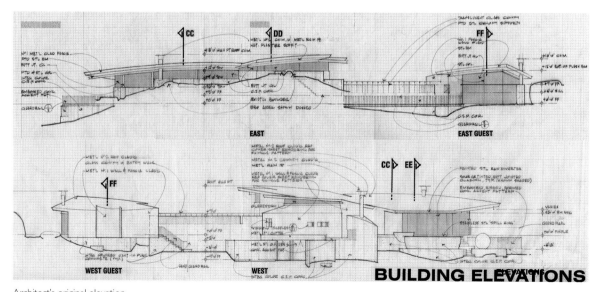

Architect's original elevation.

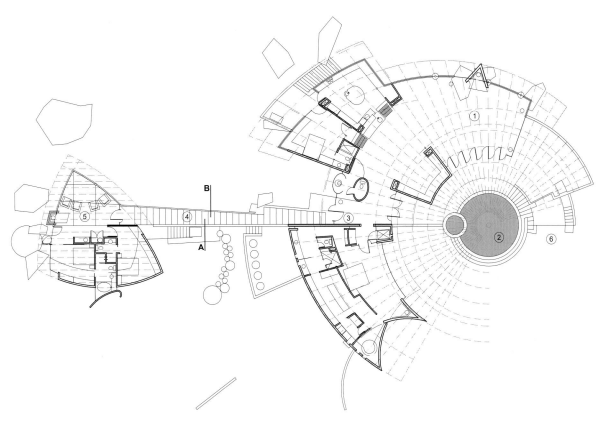

PLAN

① GREAT ROOM

② POOL AND SPA

③ MAIN ENTRY

④ ARCADE

⑤ GUEST HOUSE

⑥ SCULPTURE DECK

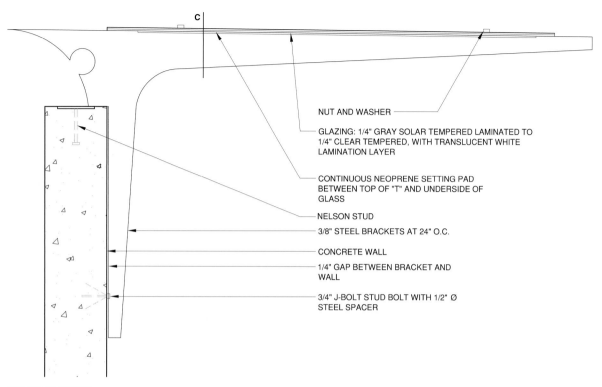

C

NUT AND WASHER

GLAZING: 1/4" GRAY SOLAR TEMPERED LAMINATED TO
1/4" CLEAR TEMPERED, WITH TRANSLUCENT WHITE
LAMINATION LAYER

CONTINUOUS NEOPRENE SETTING PAD
BETWEEN TOP OF "T" AND UNDERSIDE OF
GLASS

NELSON STUD

3/8" STEEL BRACKETS AT 24" O.C.

CONCRETE WALL

1/4" GAP BETWEEN BRACKET AND
WALL

3/4" J-BOLT STUD BOLT WITH 1/2" Ø
STEEL SPACER

**SECTION A: CANOPY
DETAIL**

The assembly shelters
guests from sun and
wind. The 7-foot-tall
concrete wall supports
the brackets that, in
turn, support the
glass canopy. The
brackets are spaced
at 24 inches on center.
The concrete forms
were laid at 48 inches.
Holding the brackets
1/4 inch off the wall
allows a narrow reveal.

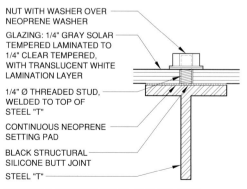

NUT WITH WASHER OVER
NEOPRENE WASHER

GLAZING: 1/4" GRAY SOLAR
TEMPERED LAMINATED TO
1/4" CLEAR TEMPERED,
WITH TRANSLUCENT WHITE
LAMINATION LAYER

1/4" Ø THREADED STUD,
WELDED TO TOP OF
STEEL "T"

CONTINUOUS NEOPRENE
SETTING PAD

BLACK STRUCTURAL
SILICONE BUTT JOINT

STEEL "T"

SECTION C: FASTENER DETAIL AT GLASS JOINT

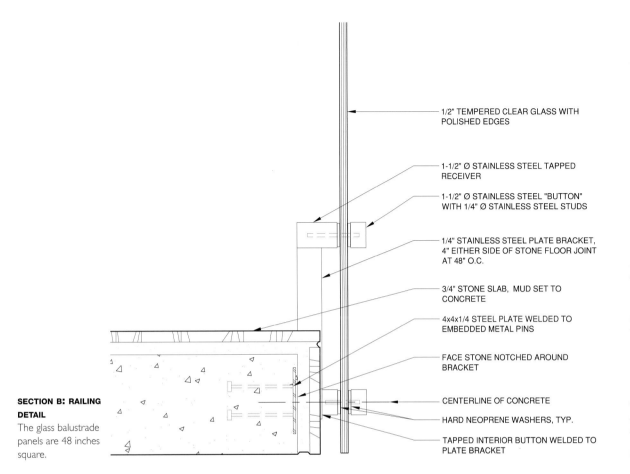

1/2" TEMPERED CLEAR GLASS WITH POLISHED EDGES

1-1/2" Ø STAINLESS STEEL TAPPED RECEIVER

1-1/2" Ø STAINLESS STEEL "BUTTON" WITH 1/4" Ø STAINLESS STEEL STUDS

1/4" STAINLESS STEEL PLATE BRACKET, 4" EITHER SIDE OF STONE FLOOR JOINT AT 48" O.C.

3/4" STONE SLAB, MUD SET TO CONCRETE

4x4x1/4 STEEL PLATE WELDED TO EMBEDDED METAL PINS

FACE STONE NOTCHED AROUND BRACKET

CENTERLINE OF CONCRETE

HARD NEOPRENE WASHERS, TYP.

TAPPED INTERIOR BUTTON WELDED TO PLATE BRACKET

SECTION B: RAILING DETAIL

The glass balustrade panels are 48 inches square.

Trenton Central Fire Headquarters and Museum, Trenton, New Jersey

Venturi, Scott Brown and Associates, Inc. with The Vaughn Collaborative, Associated Architect, and M.K.N. Associates

Bold sign graphics announce a public entrance at a working fire headquarters and museum

Since publication of the book *Learning from Las Vegas*, Venturi, Scott Brown and Associates, have raised the question, "Is signage architecture?" At the Trenton Central Fire Headquarters, signage is decidedly part of the architecture, where it announces the building's identity and the main entry to a public museum. The literalism of the headquarters' fire-hat symbol helps it stand out in its location near a major highway. And there is a tradition of signs in Trenton: The city's best-known landmark is an illuminated slogan erected in 1911 on a Delaware River bridge that reads, "TRENTON MAKES THE WORLD TAKES."

This addition is to a firehouse that dates from the early 1900s and is now a museum. The project includes an active fire company, a repair shop, administrative headquarters, and maintenance facilities. The signage provides continuity for the long, low building and turns what is an otherwise standard facility into a place of civic pride.

The helmet and the letters are powder-coated ¼-inch steel plate outlined with channel. The plate is set back 2¼ inches from the edge of the channel, creating a reveal. Neon lighting, set into the channel, outlines the letters and the helmet in a bluish white light at night.

All of the sign's components are similarly mounted, though their distance from the building wall varies as the façade jogs along. The hat, for example, is approximately 8 feet from the building face, while the letters along the on-duty station are about 2 feet from the building. The sign elements are situated on 8-inch-diameter painted piping. The piping is welded to anchorage tubing that goes through the brick face and connects to backup structural steel approximately every 20 feet.

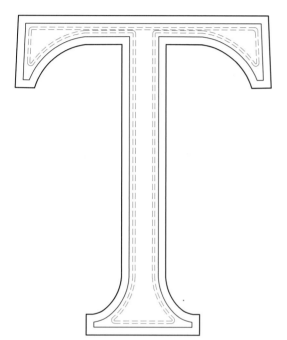

TYPICAL ELEVATION: LETTER

For visual continuity, a piece of 1-foot, 7-inch steel plate forms a stripe that runs behind the letters and the helmet. Letters are bolted to the stripe and to tubes at top and bottom.

Matt Wargo for Venturi, Scott Brown and Associates, Inc.

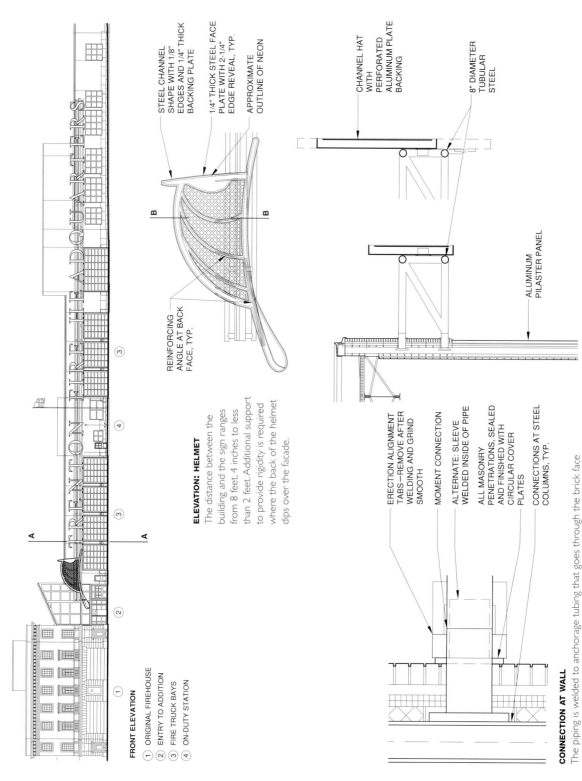

TRENTON FIRE HEADQUARTERS

FRONT ELEVATION

① ORIGINAL FIREHOUSE
② ENTRY TO ADDITION
③ FIRE TRUCK BAYS
④ ON-DUTY STATION

ELEVATION: HELMET

The distance between the building and the sign ranges from 8 feet, 4 inches to less than 2 feet. Additional support to provide rigidity is required where the back of the helmet dips over the facade.

STEEL CHANNEL SHAPE WITH 1/8" EDGES AND 1/4" THICK BACKING PLATE

1/4" THICK STEEL FACE PLATE WITH 2-1/4" EDGE REVEAL, TYP.

APPROXIMATE OUTLINE OF NEON

REINFORCING ANGLE AT BACK FACE, TYP.

CHANNEL HAT WITH PERFORATED ALUMINUM PLATE BACKING

8" DIAMETER TUBULAR STEEL

ALUMINUM PILASTER PANEL

SECTION AA

ERECTION ALIGNMENT TABS—REMOVE AFTER WELDING AND GRIND SMOOTH

MOMENT CONNECTION

ALTERNATE: SLEEVE WELDED INSIDE OF PIPE

ALL MASONRY PENETRATIONS, SEALED AND FINISHED WITH CIRCULAR COVER PLATES

CONNECTIONS AT STEEL COLUMNS, TYP.

CONNECTION AT WALL

The piping is welded to anchorage tubing that goes through the brick face and connects to backup structural steel approximately every 20 feet.

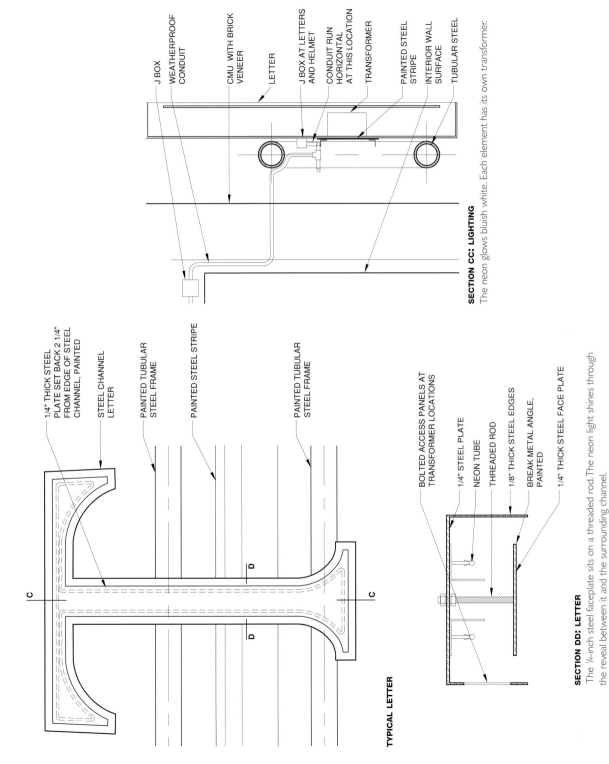

J BOX

WEATHERPROOF CONDUIT

CMU WITH BRICK VENEER

LETTER

J BOX AT LETTERS AND HELMET

CONDUIT RUN HORIZONTAL AT THIS LOCATION

TRANSFORMER

PAINTED STEEL STRIPE

INTERIOR WALL SURFACE

TUBULAR STEEL

SECTION CC: LIGHTING

The neon glows bluish white. Each element has its own transformer.

1/4" THICK STEEL PLATE SET BACK 2 1/4" FROM EDGE OF STEEL CHANNEL, PAINTED

STEEL CHANNEL LETTER

PAINTED TUBULAR STEEL FRAME

PAINTED STEEL STRIPE

PAINTED TUBULAR STEEL FRAME

TYPICAL LETTER

BOLTED ACCESS PANELS AT TRANSFORMER LOCATIONS

1/4" STEEL PLATE

NEON TUBE

THREADED ROD

1/8" THICK STEEL EDGES

BREAK METAL ANGLE, PAINTED

1/4" THICK STEEL FACE PLATE

SECTION DD: LETTER

The ¼-inch steel faceplate sits on a threaded rod. The neon light shines through the reveal between it and the surrounding channel.

Trenton Central Fire Headquarters and Museum, Trenton, New Jersey   83

INTERIOR TRANSITIONS

Timothy Hursley.

Timothy Hursley.

The Crystal Grotto at the Mii amo Spa in Sedona, Arizona, is a place of crystals, earth, water, and quiet; a place to commune with the elements and get in touch with your soul. Visitors enter through a tunnel designed by **Gluckman Mayner Architects** that is made of indigenous alder wood and arches across a 6-inch-deep pool of water.

If the entry to the Crystal Grotto takes people away to a spiritual place, **Diller Scofidio + Renfro's** entry

Harry Zernike.

to The Brasserie in Mies van der Rohe's Seagram Building in New York City plunks them squarely in the middle of the social scene. The see-and-be-seen entry guides diners from the hostess, who stands on the entry's "landing platform," to a gradual glass stairway that ends in the center of the dining room. The secret of this sophisticated stair is a carefully designed stainless steel stringer that supports the 4-foot-tall glass railing and contains channels for the risers and the treads.

Jones Studio, Inc., found a clever way to bring light through the entry to the master bedroom at the Jones-Johnson Residence in Phoenix. The glass-floored entry is positioned directly beneath a skylight that runs along the spine of the house, keeping the innermost portions of the house bright all day long. It was important that the flow of light not be interrupted by a solid door. The architect reconciled the problem by using a glass door that swings from a minimal frame that is embedded in glass.

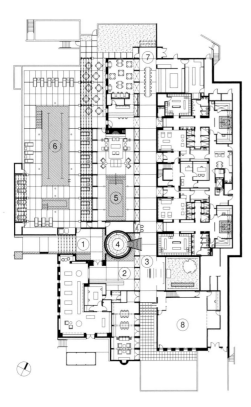

PLAN

① ENTRY COURTYARD

② LOBBY

③ HALL

④ CRYSTAL GROTTO

⑤ INDOOR POOL

⑥ OUTDOOR POOL

⑦ CAFE

⑧ FITNESS

Mii amo Spa at Enchantment Resort, Sedona, Arizona

Gluckman Mayner Architects

The tunnel entry to the Crystal Grotto at the Mii amo Spa in Sedona, Arizona, reinterprets Native American architecture.

Gluckman Mayner Architects were asked by the owners of the Mii amo Spa at Enchantment Resort to create a new spa adjacent to an existing hotel that is derivative of Native American architecture, but not imitative. To help them in their efforts, a Native American medicine man reviewed their drawings and blessed them. When the project was complete, the medicine man stood in the megaphonelike bridge entry to the spa's Crystal Grotto and delivered his invocation.

The dome-shaped grotto is the spiritual center of the spa. It is there that ceremonies honoring the sacred earth elements are held. It is also a place of crystals, earth, water, and quiet.

The entrance to the grotto is a transitional space, from corporal to spiritual. It recalls the tunnel entries to traditional Native American *kivas*—typically underground chambers used for assembly or ceremony. The dramatic, square-mouthed tunnel leads from the bright public spaces to a cavern lit by a single circle of natural light (see sidebar "Skylight or Smoke Hole?," p. 90). The floor of the tunnel arches across a 6-inch-deep pool of water, giving a greater sense of crossing a threshold. The public side of the tunnel is 8 feet wide, while the grotto side narrows to a width of about 3 feet. It is 10 feet long.

The tunnel is made of indigenous alder wood. It was fabricated off-site and slipped into the opening in the grotto like a wedge. The tongue-and-groove flooring is supported by two wood joists and 3-by-6-inch wood sills. The sills also support five 3-by-3-inch wood posts on either side and 3-by-6-inch beams across the ceiling. The walls are alder-veneer plywood.

Harry Zernike.

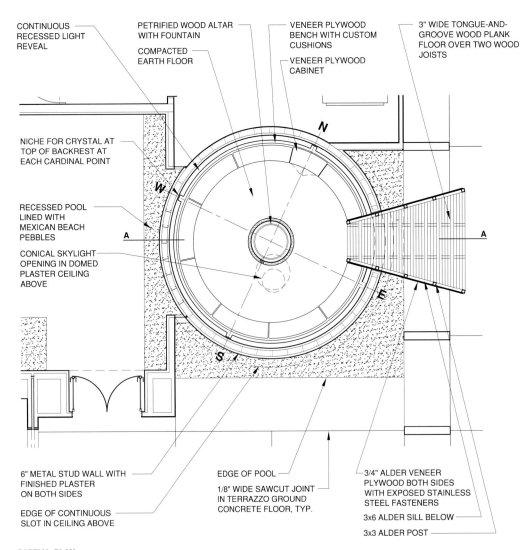

CONTINUOUS
RECESSED LIGHT
REVEAL

PETRIFIED WOOD ALTAR
WITH FOUNTAIN

COMPACTED
EARTH FLOOR

VENEER PLYWOOD
BENCH WITH CUSTOM
CUSHIONS

VENEER PLYWOOD
CABINET

3" WIDE TONGUE-AND-
GROOVE WOOD PLANK
FLOOR OVER TWO WOOD
JOISTS

NICHE FOR CRYSTAL AT
TOP OF BACKREST AT
EACH CARDINAL POINT

RECESSED POOL
LINED WITH
MEXICAN BEACH
PEBBLES

CONICAL SKYLIGHT
OPENING IN DOMED
PLASTER CEILING
ABOVE

N

W

A

S

E

A

6" METAL STUD WALL WITH
FINISHED PLASTER
ON BOTH SIDES

EDGE OF CONTINUOUS
SLOT IN CEILING ABOVE

EDGE OF POOL

1/8" WIDE SAWCUT JOINT
IN TERRAZZO GROUND
CONCRETE FLOOR, TYP.

3/4" ALDER VENEER
PLYWOOD BOTH SIDES
WITH EXPOSED STAINLESS
STEEL FASTENERS

3x6 ALDER SILL BELOW

3x3 ALDER POST

PARTIAL PLAN
The floor of the tunnel arcs over a narrow span of water and lands on an earthen floor in the grotto.

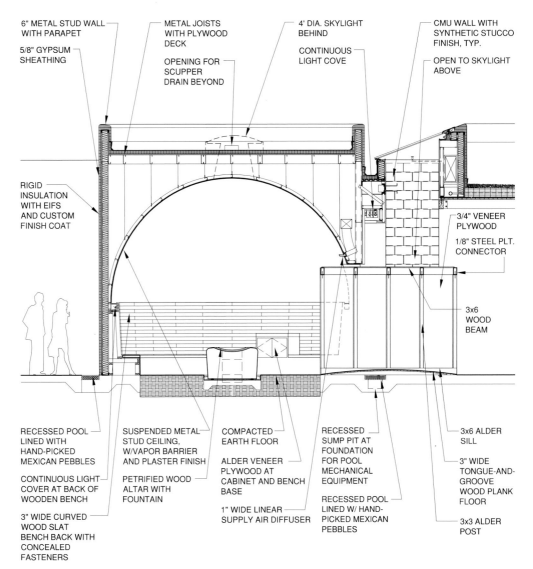

6" METAL STUD WALL WITH PARAPET

5/8" GYPSUM SHEATHING

METAL JOISTS WITH PLYWOOD DECK

OPENING FOR SCUPPER DRAIN BEYOND

4' DIA. SKYLIGHT BEHIND

CONTINUOUS LIGHT COVE

CMU WALL WITH SYNTHETIC STUCCO FINISH, TYP.

OPEN TO SKYLIGHT ABOVE

RIGID INSULATION WITH EIFS AND CUSTOM FINISH COAT

3/4" VENEER PLYWOOD

1/8" STEEL PLT. CONNECTOR

3x6 WOOD BEAM

RECESSED POOL LINED WITH HAND-PICKED MEXICAN PEBBLES

CONTINUOUS LIGHT COVER AT BACK OF WOODEN BENCH

3" WIDE CURVED WOOD SLAT BENCH BACK WITH CONCEALED FASTENERS

SUSPENDED METAL STUD CEILING, W/VAPOR BARRIER AND PLASTER FINISH

PETRIFIED WOOD ALTAR WITH FOUNTAIN

COMPACTED EARTH FLOOR

ALDER VENEER PLYWOOD AT CABINET AND BENCH BASE

1" WIDE LINEAR SUPPLY AIR DIFFUSER

RECESSED SUMP PIT AT FOUNDATION FOR POOL MECHANICAL EQUIPMENT

RECESSED POOL LINED W/ HAND-PICKED MEXICAN PEBBLES

3x6 ALDER SILL

3" WIDE TONGUE-AND-GROOVE WOOD PLANK FLOOR

3x3 ALDER POST

SECTION

The shallow pool is lined with black stones to make it appear deeper. The hand-finished stucco walls of the grotto are Prussian blue.

The walls inside the cylindrical grotto are stucco. A circular skylight illuminates the small space and, on the summer solstice, directs sunlight on the petrified-wood altar at the center. *Harry Zernike.*

Skylight or Smoke Hole?

Each year at noon on June 21 the sun shines through the circular skylight in the Crystal Grotto, tracks across the earthen floor, and illuminates an altar made of petrified wood and crystal in the center of the room. While the skylight is large enough that the sunbeam didn't need to be pinpoint accurate, it still needed to be properly positioned.

The architect started by running a series of astronomical calculations based on textbook longitude and latitude estimates. When they got on-site and tried to verify these with a magnetic compass, their numbers were off. "We finally realized that one of the unique things about Sedona is its magnetic anomalies," says project architect Gregory Yang. "We threw away the compass measurements and relied on Global Positioning System services."

The owners of the spa also wanted the skylight to look like a smoke hole in a traditional kiva. To accomplish this, Gluckman Mayner capped the tapered shaft with a standard skylight system, but set its framing structure outside the perimeter of the shaft on the surrounding flat roof. A parapet hides the top of the skylight from view.

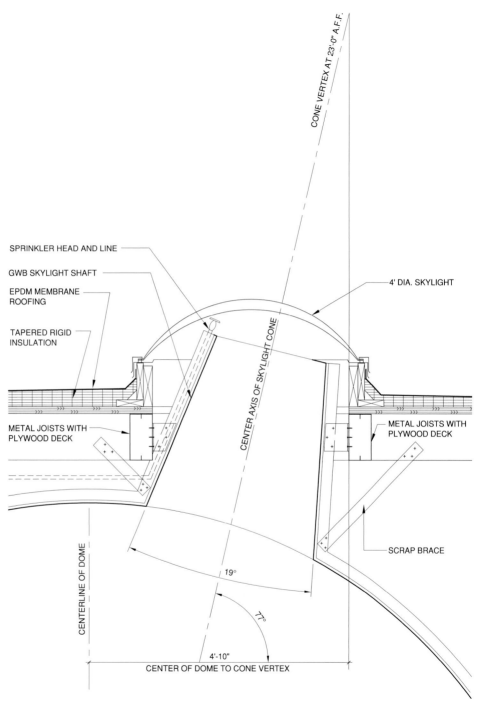

CONE VERTEX AT 23'-0" A.F.F.

SPRINKLER HEAD AND LINE

GWB SKYLIGHT SHAFT

EPDM MEMBRANE ROOFING

TAPERED RIGID INSULATION

4' DIA. SKYLIGHT

CENTER AXIS OF SKYLIGHT CONE

METAL JOISTS WITH PLYWOOD DECK

METAL JOISTS WITH PLYWOOD DECK

SCRAP BRACE

CENTERLINE OF DOME

19°

7°

4'-10"

CENTER OF DOME TO CONE VERTEX

SKYLIGHT SECTION

The cone-shaped skylight is not visible from the exterior of the building.

The Brasserie, Seagram Building, New York City, New York

Diller Scofidio + Renfro

A slick entry to a hip restaurant in the basement of Mies van der Rohe's Seagram Building is more theater than ingress.

Diller Scofidio + Renfro were presented with what amounted to a plain concrete box that could not be altered because of the Seagram Building's landmark status, so their strategy employed built-up layers of pear wood that were molded to create a sculptural interior shell. A long, gradual entry stair breaches the shell, dramatically landing visitors in the center of the restaurant.

As customers step into the revolving entry door, their photo is taken by a tiny spy camera mounted on the back of the shell. The photo is transmitted to the first in a series of 15 monitors located over the bar. As new customers arrive, the most recent portrait takes the first position and racks the previous 15 to the right, dropping away the oldest. There is a delay between the time when a visitor's photo appears on the monitor and when the visitor appears on the entry stair. That "telegenic lag," says project leader Charles Renfro, "is what makes the entrance; the technology and the physical act together with dramatic results."

After checking with the hostess on the "landing platform," guests proceed to the stair. The top step and the riser beneath are, like the platform floor, Palladiana terrazzo—a style popular in the 1930s that features chunks of marble (up to 1 foot by 1 foot) mixed with smaller aggregate. On either side of the stair, a section of the wood shell arcs up to the ceiling, while another piece slips down to form a bench where diners sit. These pieces meet at supporting steel ribs, visible at either side of the stair. The ribs are bolted to floor.

The stainless steel stringer hangs on the steel beams that support the entry platform. Channels at either edge of the stringer support the 4-foot-tall glass railing. The handrails on either side were originally intended to be long, slender pieces of wood, but these were abandoned when the architect realized they wouldn't meet code. Instead, the rail is stainless steel with custom-cast end pieces that cantilever into the room, prolonging the stair's run.

The glass risers, which help support the treads above, and the treads consist of dual layers of laminated glass. The risers slip into channels in the stringer; these same channels serve as ledges to support the treads. The risers are 4 inches tall and treads are 17 inches deep, making for a gradual descent and giving other diners plenty of time to see who's coming. A brief set of stairs at the side of the landing platform is provided for those who prefer a surreptitious entry.

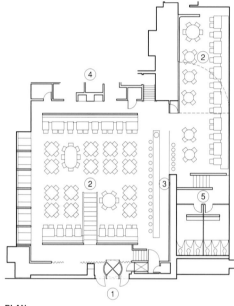

PLAN

1. ENTRY
2. DINING ROOM
3. BAR
4. KITCHEN
5. RESTROOMS

The entry stair has a 4:17 run, making for a very gradual, dramatic descent into the restaurant's dining room. *Michael Moran.*

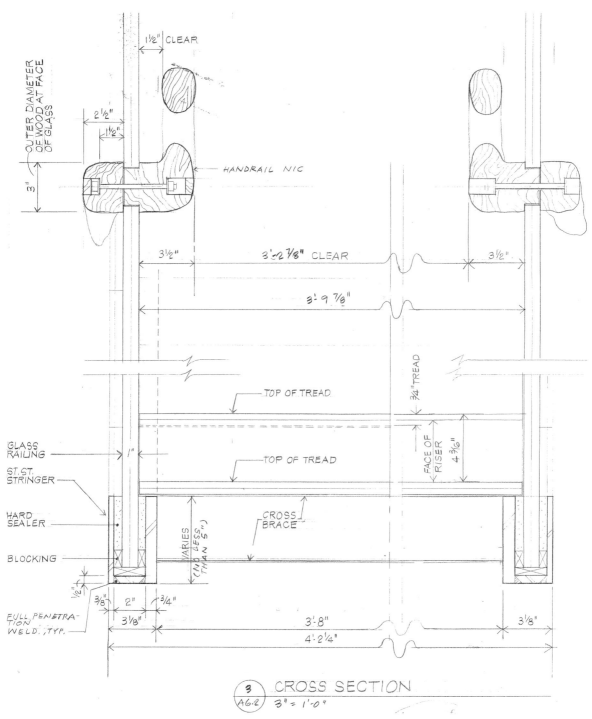

1½" CLEAR

OUTER DIAMETER OF WOOD AT FACE OF GLASS

2½"

1½"

3"

HANDRAIL NIC

3½"

3'-2 7/8" CLEAR

3½"

3'-9 7/8"

3/4" TREAD

TOP OF TREAD

FACE OF RISER

4 3/16"

GLASS RAILING

1"

TOP OF TREAD

ST. ST. STRINGER

HARD SEALER

BLOCKING

VARIES (NO LESS THAN 5")

CROSS BRACE

½"

3/8"

2"

3/4"

FULL PENETRA- TION WELD., TYP.

3 1/8"

3'-8"

4'-2 1/4"

3 1/8"

3 CROSS SECTION
A6.2 3" = 1'-0"

ARCHITECT'S ORIGINAL DRAWINGS
SECTION DETAIL: STAIR AND RAILING
Handrails were originally to be made from slender pieces of wood but were changed to stainless steel because of code limitations.

The 1-inch-thick pear-veneered shell pieces join at a steel rib. To make the pear wood shell glow, fluorescent lamps were set between the overlapping layers of wood. *Michael Moran.*

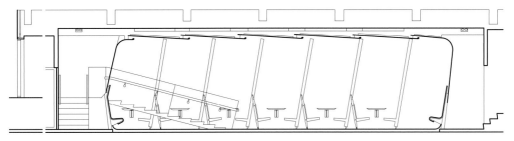

SECTION: DINING ROOM

ARCHITECT'S STUDY OF ENTRY STAIR SECTION

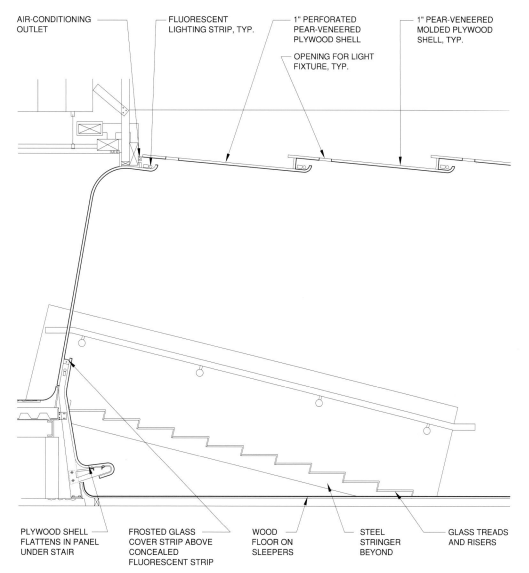

AIR-CONDITIONING OUTLET

FLUORESCENT LIGHTING STRIP, TYP.

1" PERFORATED PEAR-VENEERED PLYWOOD SHELL

1" PEAR-VENEERED MOLDED PLYWOOD SHELL, TYP.

OPENING FOR LIGHT FIXTURE, TYP.

PLYWOOD SHELL FLATTENS IN PANEL UNDER STAIR

FROSTED GLASS COVER STRIP ABOVE CONCEALED FLUORESCENT STRIP

WOOD FLOOR ON SLEEPERS

STEEL STRINGER BEYOND

GLASS TREADS AND RISERS

LONGITUDINAL SECTION

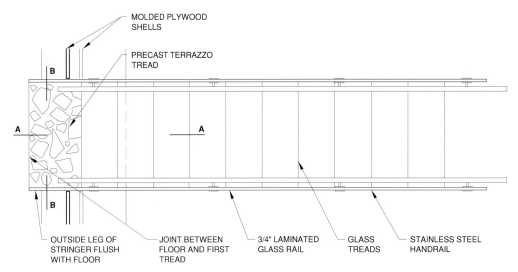

MOLDED PLYWOOD
SHELLS

PRECAST TERRAZZO
TREAD

B

A — — A

B

OUTSIDE LEG OF
STRINGER FLUSH
WITH FLOOR

JOINT BETWEEN
FLOOR AND FIRST
TREAD

3/4" LAMINATED
GLASS RAIL

GLASS
TREADS

STAINLESS STEEL
HANDRAIL

ENTRY STAIR PLAN

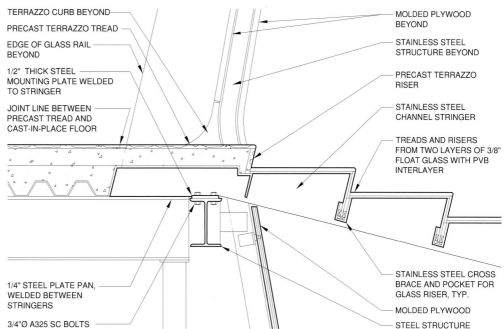

TERRAZZO CURB BEYOND

PRECAST TERRAZZO TREAD

EDGE OF GLASS RAIL BEYOND

1/2" THICK STEEL MOUNTING PLATE WELDED TO STRINGER

JOINT LINE BETWEEN PRECAST TREAD AND CAST-IN-PLACE FLOOR

MOLDED PLYWOOD BEYOND

STAINLESS STEEL STRUCTURE BEYOND

PRECAST TERRAZZO RISER

STAINLESS STEEL CHANNEL STRINGER

TREADS AND RISERS FROM TWO LAYERS OF 3/8" FLOAT GLASS WITH PVB INTERLAYER

STAINLESS STEEL CROSS BRACE AND POCKET FOR GLASS RISER, TYP.

MOLDED PLYWOOD

STEEL STRUCTURE

SECTION AA: LANDING AND STAIR

The custom-fabricated stringer hangs from steel beams beneath the landing platform.

1/4" STEEL PLATE PAN, WELDED BETWEEN STRINGERS

3/4"Ø A325 SC BOLTS

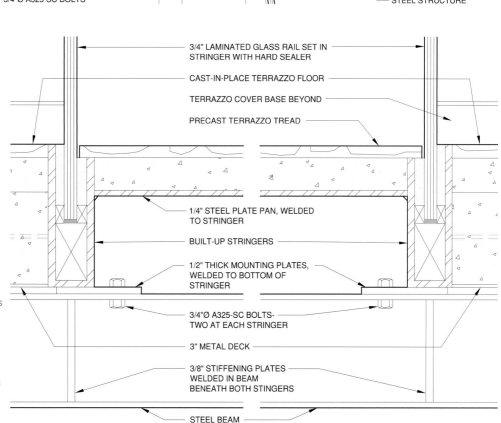

3/4" LAMINATED GLASS RAIL SET IN STRINGER WITH HARD SEALER

CAST-IN-PLACE TERRAZZO FLOOR

TERRAZZO COVER BASE BEYOND

PRECAST TERRAZZO TREAD

1/4" STEEL PLATE PAN, WELDED TO STRINGER

BUILT-UP STRINGERS

1/2" THICK MOUNTING PLATES, WELDED TO BOTTOM OF STRINGER

3/4"Ø A325-SC BOLTS- TWO AT EACH STRINGER

3" METAL DECK

3/8" STIFFENING PLATES WELDED IN BEAM BENEATH BOTH STRINGERS

STEEL BEAM

SECTION BB: LANDING

The glass railing rests in a pocket that runs the length of the stringer. Wood blocking and sealant prevents any movement. The glass railing is tempered and laminated for safety.

The Brasserie, Seagram Building, New York City, New York 99

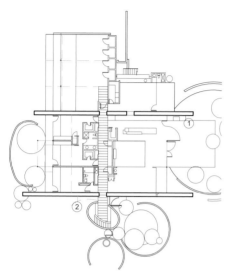

LOWER-LEVEL PLAN

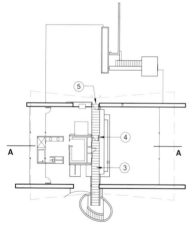

UPPER-LEVEL PLAN

① ENTRY

② STAIR TO SECOND FLOOR

③ GLASS-FLOORED CORRIDOR

④ ENTRY TO MASTER BEDROOM

⑤ BALCONY DOOR

Jones Residence, Phoenix, Arizona

Jones Studio, Inc.

A door floating in glass allows natural light to permeate a rammed-earth house.

Jones Studio, Inc., principal Eddie Jones, AIA, focused on natural light and ventilation when designing this rammed-earth house for his family. A central corridor organizes the two-story house, dividing public and private space. Careful solar orientation, together with a skylight bisecting the roof from east to west and a glass floor running the length of the corridor, keep the innermost portions of the house bright all day long.

Positioning solid doors along the second-story corridor would have interfered with the flow of light, yet a door was needed to separate the master bedroom from the study area. So Jones came up with a way to minimize solid wood members, maximize glass, and support the 3-by-8-foot door.

Both the skylight and the glass floor are supported by clear fir 2-by-10 cross members set at 16 inches on center. These cross members run parallel to one another and are routed, like furniture, into hefty glulams at either side.

The door frame appears to be sitting on glass, but the vertical members are doweled into the parallel 2-by-10 cross members above and below. The 1-by-4 door header is also routed into the glulams it straddles. The header also serves as a conduit, carrying wiring across the skylight.

The door is flanked by 1/4-inch tempered glass. This is routed into the door frame and the rammed-earth wall, and, at floor level, slipped into a joint in the 1-inch-thick glass. It also abuts the drywall in some places and is held with clear silicone stops.

Timothy Hursley.

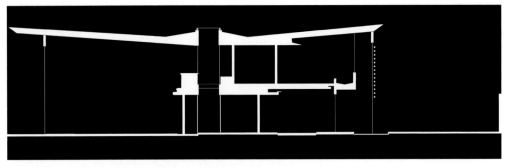

ARCHITECT'S FIGURE—GROUND STUDY

A glass-floored, upper-level corridor is aligned with a skylight that bisects the roof from east to west. Daylight penetrating the two levels of glass brightens the innermost portions of the house.

View from the glass floor of the upper-level corridor. *Timothy Hursley.*

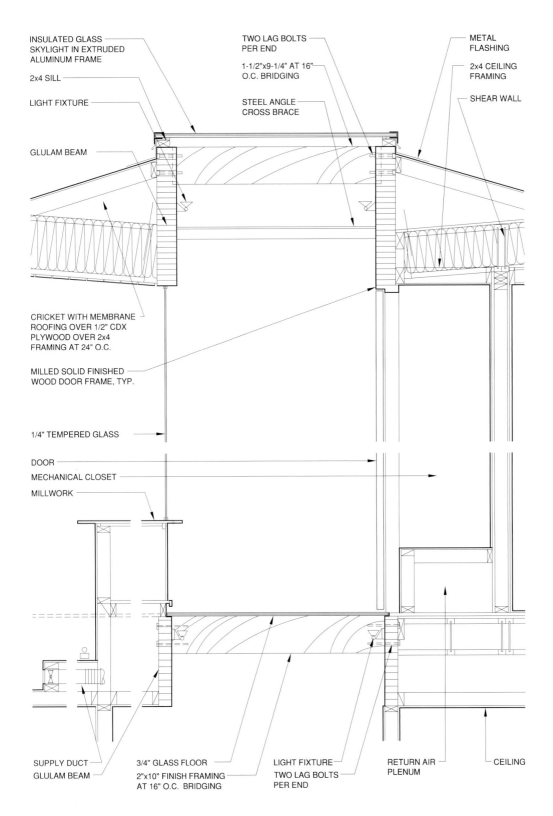

INSULATED GLASS
SKYLIGHT IN EXTRUDED
ALUMINUM FRAME

2x4 SILL

LIGHT FIXTURE

GLULAM BEAM

TWO LAG BOLTS
PER END

1-1/2"x9-1/4" AT 16"
O.C. BRIDGING

STEEL ANGLE
CROSS BRACE

METAL
FLASHING

2x4 CEILING
FRAMING

SHEAR WALL

CRICKET WITH MEMBRANE
ROOFING OVER 1/2" CDX
PLYWOOD OVER 2x4
FRAMING AT 24" O.C.

MILLED SOLID FINISHED
WOOD DOOR FRAME, TYP.

1/4" TEMPERED GLASS

DOOR

MECHANICAL CLOSET

MILLWORK

SUPPLY DUCT
GLULAM BEAM

3/4" GLASS FLOOR
2"x10" FINISH FRAMING
AT 16" O.C. BRIDGING

LIGHT FIXTURE
TWO LAG BOLTS
PER END

RETURN AIR
PLENUM

CEILING

SECTION:

UPPER LEVEL

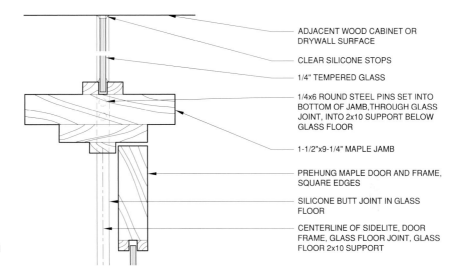

MASTER BEDROOM DOOR: HEAD/JAMB DETAIL
The 1/4-inch tempered glass at either side of the door is routed into the door frame and rests in a slot in the glass floor. It is held in place with silicone.

ADJACENT WOOD CABINET OR DRYWALL SURFACE

CLEAR SILICONE STOPS

1/4" TEMPERED GLASS

1/4x6 ROUND STEEL PINS SET INTO BOTTOM OF JAMB, THROUGH GLASS JOINT, INTO 2x10 SUPPORT BELOW GLASS FLOOR

1-1/2"x9-1/4" MAPLE JAMB

PREHUNG MAPLE DOOR AND FRAME, SQUARE EDGES

SILICONE BUTT JOINT IN GLASS FLOOR

CENTERLINE OF SIDELITE, DOOR FRAME, GLASS FLOOR JOINT, GLASS FLOOR 2x10 SUPPORT

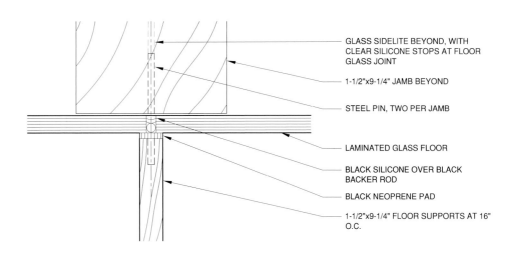

SILL DETAIL
Door/frame not shown for clarity.

GLASS SIDELITE BEYOND, WITH CLEAR SILICONE STOPS AT FLOOR GLASS JOINT

1-1/2"x9-1/4" JAMB BEYOND

STEEL PIN, TWO PER JAMB

LAMINATED GLASS FLOOR

BLACK SILICONE OVER BLACK BACKER ROD

BLACK NEOPRENE PAD

1-1/2"x9-1/4" FLOOR SUPPORTS AT 16" O.C.

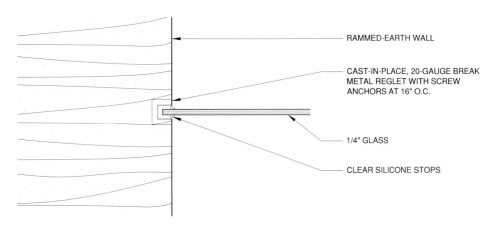

DETAIL: GLASS AT WALL

RAMMED-EARTH WALL

CAST-IN-PLACE, 20-GAUGE BREAK METAL REGLET WITH SCREW ANCHORS AT 16" O.C.

1/4" GLASS

CLEAR SILICONE STOPS

CANOPIES

Chuck Choi Architectural Photography.

Chuck Choi Architectural Photography.

Glass canopies abound, but few are as highly engineered as the glass-and-steel canopy at the Marriott East in New York City. Designed by **Perkins Eastman Architects** with **Advanced Structures Inc.,** the Marriott canopy extends more than 58 feet in length and projects 14 feet over the city sidewalk. It includes upper and lower stainless steel catenary cables that, together, hold the structure in tension.

Smith-Miller + Hawkinson Architects' delicate structure at the Corning Museum of Glass in Corning, New York, by comparison, is strikingly simple. It features two sections of glass that pivot off a central column like the wings of a butterfly. Each wing is made from 4-by-6-foot sheets of 3/8-inch tempered glass that rest upon upside-down T-shaped steel bars.

Paul Warchol.

Entrance Canopy for Marriott East, New York City, New York

Perkins Eastman Architects

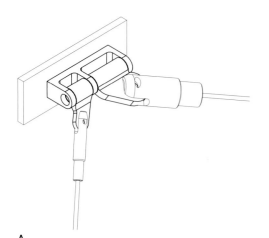

A
CABLE ANCHORAGE AT FACADE

Contact with the limestone façade was minimized with tiebacks like this one. It connects the cables, top and bottom, at four points. The tiebacks are located in front of steel structural members. *Chuck Choi Architectural Photography.*

A broad, highly engineered canopy shelters guests and doormen at the Marriott East in New York City.

Perkins Eastman Architects with Advanced Structures Inc. were inspired by nineteenth-century glass-and-steel canopies when creating this bow-shaped structure, part of a major renovation of a 1920s hotel. The canopy glass slips around the entrance colonnade, preserving the existing limestone façade and minimizing building contact. The assembly extends more than 58 feet in length and projects 14 feet over the city sidewalk.

Sections of ³/₄-inch tempered laminated glass are arrayed below a 12-by-4-inch, 60-foot-long arching steel tube. This connects to a 6-inch-diameter steel tube that is flush with the façade and runs the full length of the canopy. The resulting bow-shaped superstructure terminates at either end with a pin-shaped connector that slips into a wall-mounted bracket. The pins have some room to rotate, allowing the canopy a small amount of movement.

The superstructure is held in position between upper and lower stainless steel catenary cables. The upper catenary carries the dead load, while the lower one counteracts uplift. Both cables are anchored at two points on the façade with custom clevis plates that enable limited movement. The top cable is attached to the arch superstructure. The lower cable is attached to the lower spreader bar. The two cables are connected via a ³/₄-inch carbon steel plate suspended from the arch. The stainless steel plate also serves as the connection for the radiating fins.

The glass panels are suspended from two-pronged fittings attached at 18- to 24-inch intervals along stainless steel fins. Each fin, made from two layers of ¹/₂-inch stainless steel, is shaped differently, depending upon its location on the canopy. The fins are attached to the superstructure by the ³/₄-inch plates attached to the arch and via a tail plate fitted around the circular tube at the façade. The tail plate connection is designed to allow for the radiating differently angled connection at each fin. Small glass fins, roughly 28 inches in length, are sandwiched between the steel fins and extend, like fingernails, along the outside edge of the canopy, making the structure appear light and transparent.

Chuck Choi Architectural Photography.

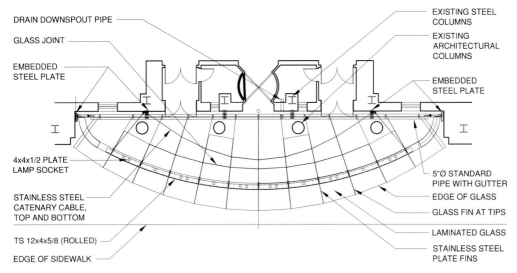

PLAN

The canopy's supporting steel arch is attached to the building in two places. Custom connectors tie the canopy to the building's structural steel.

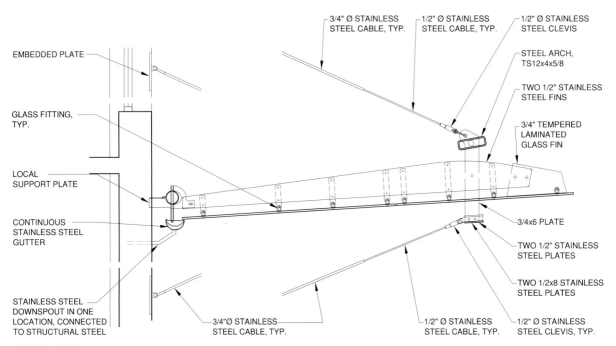

SECTION AT FIN

Glass tips rimming the canopy top resemble fingernails. Electrical wiring for lighting and heaters runs along the top of the 4-by-6 steel arch. Radial cables (top and bottom) are ½ inch in diameter and are connected with knuckle fittings to the catenary cables, which vary in diameter depending on the load they are carrying.

The new glass-and-steel canopy, which replaces one made of brown canvas, stands 14 feet off the sidewalk. It is held in tension by top and bottom catenary cables. The glass is slotted around the building's nonstructural limestone columns. It has a 60 percent ceramic frit, which makes the glass more reflective and keeps it looking cleaner. *Chuck Choi Architectural Photography*.

Entrance Canopy for Marriott East, New York City, New York 111

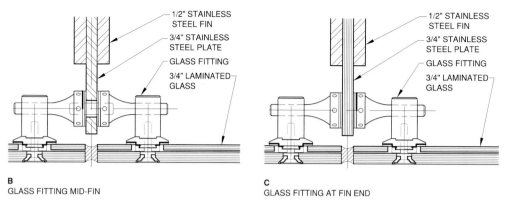

B
GLASS FITTING MID-FIN

C
GLASS FITTING AT FIN END

The fins are shaped differently as they fan out around the canopy top. The fin assembly comprises two ½-inch stainless steel plates. The double plates allow for all the connections to be made between and through the fin. The connection to the superstructure is made via the ¾-inch plate attached to the arch and a "tail plate." The glass fittings are also connected with plates.

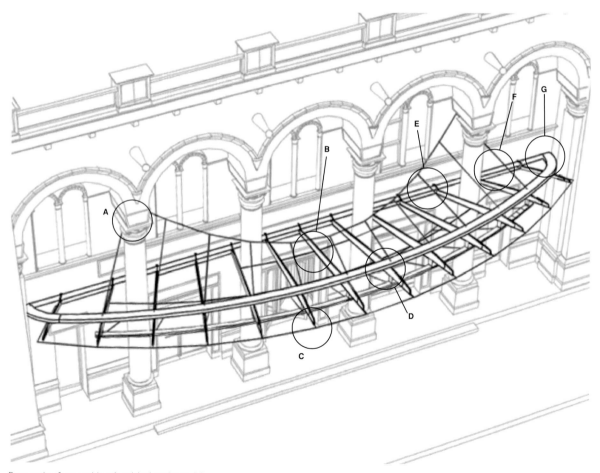

Perspective from architect's original study model.

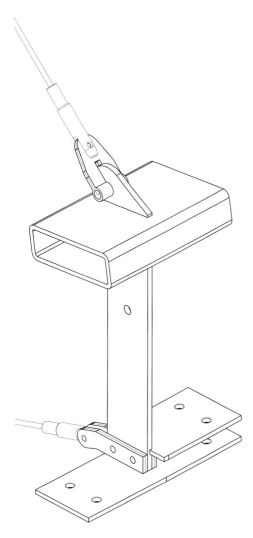

D
CABLE CONNECTIONS AT UPPER ARCH SUPERSTRUCTURE
AND LOWER SPREADER BAR

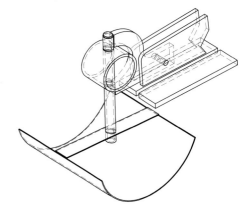

E
FIN STABILIZER WITH GUTTER

A stainless steel gutter, attached to the fittings with straps,
runs the length of the canopy and
collects water that flows off
the back of the canopy.

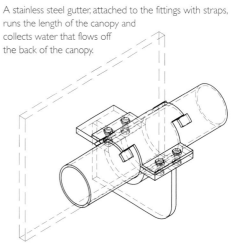

F
FACADE BRACE

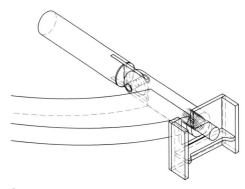

G
ARCH SUPPORT AT SIDE WALL

The 60-foot-long steel arch terminates at either end with a
pin connection. The pin rotates, giving the arch some room
to move. The cables prevent it from moving too much.

Corning Museum of Glass, Corning, New York

Smith-Miller + Hawkinson Architects

A crystalline canopy echoes a museum's fragile contents.

Smith-Miller + Hawkinson Architects' delicate canopy shelters a museum café and provides a covered walkway to the museum's jitney path. Pivoting off of a central column are two winglike sections of glass, one hugging the museum building and the other veering off in the opposite direction.

The minimal canopy, an addition to the existing building, tucks under the eaves and shelters the entry area. The wing that runs along the building is 8 feet tall; the entry doors are 7 feet, 11 inches. The angled wing is slightly taller at 8 feet, 9 inches.

Each wing is made from 4-by-6-foot sheets of $3/8$-inch tempered glass. The sheets rest upon upside-down T-shaped steel bars. The bottom of the T is 5 inches wide; the top is 8 inches tall. A layer of neoprene separates glass and steel. Only the substantial weight of the glass panels hold them in place on the T.

A steel tube running on top of the T-shaped bars on each wing holds the bars in place. The tubes are angled, though the panels are straight. The result, on both sides of the canopy, is unequal steel arms that play with perspective.

The angled edge of the canopy is welded to an existing column, located beneath the mechanical penthouse. The opposite edge attaches to the concrete underside of the jitney path with diagonal V-shaped braces made of steel tubing.

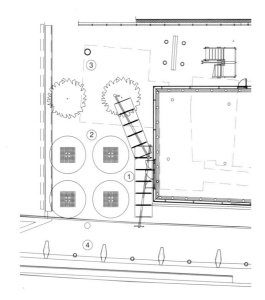

BUILDING PLAN

1. CANOPY
2. OUTDOOR CAFE
3. MECHANICAL PENTHOUSE
4. JITNEY PATH

Paul Warchol.

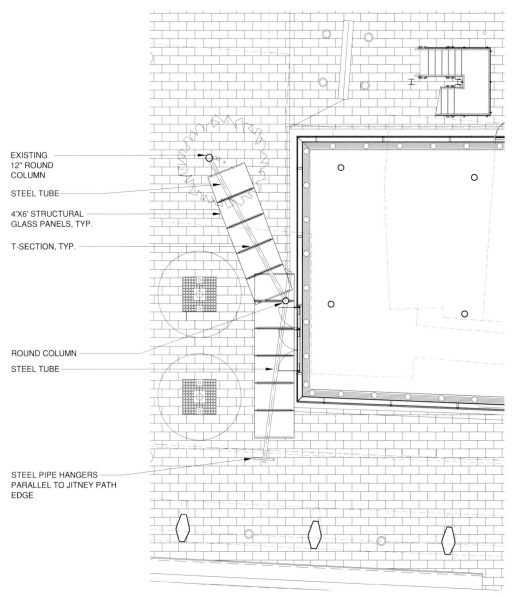

EXISTING
12" ROUND
COLUMN

STEEL TUBE

4'X6' STRUCTURAL
GLASS PANELS, TYP.

T-SECTION, TYP.

ROUND COLUMN

STEEL TUBE

STEEL PIPE HANGERS
PARALLEL TO JITNEY PATH
EDGE

PLAN

The canopy's central column follows the line of existing columns in the building. The column beneath the mechanical penthouse was in place before the canopy was added; the end of the canopy was welded to it.

The east-facing wing of the canopy is welded to the central steel column, while the western wing was bolted to allow for some play in the structure. The somewhat flexible V-shaped brackets at the end of the east-facing wing allow for some movement as well. The entire assembly is only inches above the tops of the entry doors. *Judith Turner.*

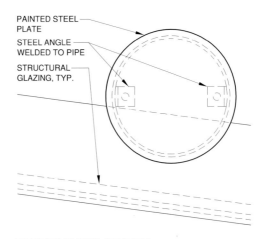

PAINTED STEEL
PLATE

STEEL ANGLE
WELDED TO PIPE

STRUCTURAL
GLAZING, TYP.

ELEVATION A: STEEL PIPE BEAM

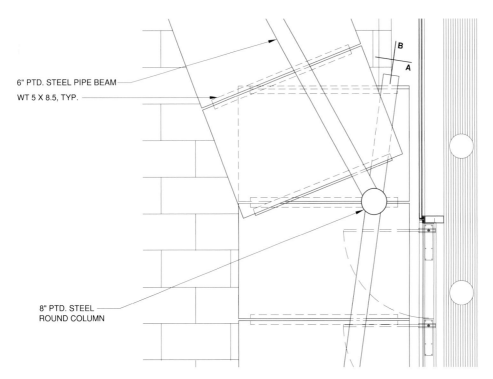

6" PTD. STEEL PIPE BEAM

WT 5 X 8.5, TYP.

8" PTD. STEEL
ROUND COLUMN

B

A

PLAN DETAIL

The wing running along the building is 4 inches from the curtain wall. The gap is sheltered by the roof above.

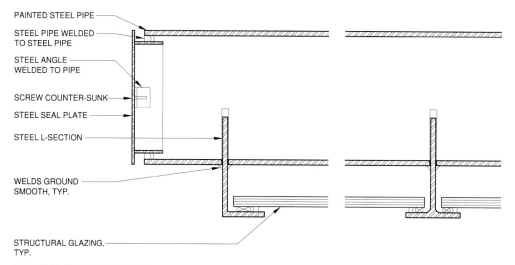

PAINTED STEEL PIPE

STEEL PIPE WELDED
TO STEEL PIPE

STEEL ANGLE
WELDED TO PIPE

SCREW COUNTER-SUNK

STEEL SEAL PLATE

STEEL L-SECTION

WELDS GROUND
SMOOTH, TYP.

STRUCTURAL GLAZING,
TYP.

SECTION B: CANOPY CONNECTION

The ends of the canopy wings rest on L-shaped steel bars. The flange of the L is 2½ inches wide; the vertical piece is 8 inches tall.

SCULPTURAL

Nick Wood.

The three original and inspiring structures in this section—**Wilkinson Eyre Architects'** complex "Bridge of Aspiration," **Obie G. Bowman's** whimsical Pins Sur Mer, and **Rural Studio Outreach's** exuberantly innovative The Lucy House—support the theory that architecture is art; though the carefulness and precision with which this art is achieved support the theory that architecture is science. And so the debate continues.

The Bridge of Aspiration spirals between The Royal Ballet School and The Royal Opera House in London. It includes an aluminum box beam that is the base for a series of 23 aluminum-and-wood hoops, each of which rotates 4 degrees. Glass inserted between the hoops at once encases the bridge and

Tim Hursley.

showcases the dancers that lightly travel its 9.5-meter span.

Bowman parks a 28-inch-diameter redwood log gutter right over the entrance to this little house in Caifornia's Mendocino County. The log is supported by four hand-hewn redwood brackets. Both elements, made of wood from a nearby mill, were made by the contractor.

The Lucy House, a project in Hale County, Alabama, is the work of a band of students assembled under the auspices of the School of Architecture at Auburn University by the late architect and teacher Samuel "Sambo" Mockbee. It is made from lowly carpet tiles that achieve unexpected beauty—and an R-value of greater than 50—as wall material. Even the laminated plywood that makes up the window frames looks good here; the layers of wood echo the layers of carpet. Best of all, the house was a way for the students to learn and understand architecture and the building process.

The Royal Ballet School "Bridge of Aspiration," London

Wilkinson Eyre Architects

A connecting pedestrian bridge pirouettes from the ballet school to The Royal Opera House.

Wilkinson Eyre Architects' footbridge links the ballet school classrooms to the much sought after Royal Opera House stage, home of The Royal Ballet. The design of the fourth-floor level bridge was constricted by the carrying capacity of the building structures. The Royal Opera House dates from 1858, though it has been refurbished frequently—the wall to which the bridge attaches is concrete poured in the 1970s. The Royal Ballet School, recently completed, is a steel structure.

The 9.5-meter span consists of 23 aluminum-and-wood hoops or portals that swirl around a complex, custom-fabricated aluminum box beam. The hoops are bolted to flanges along the underside of the aluminum beam. The beam is wide and flat at the ends, where it connects to the buildings, and deep in the center to minimize deflection. The hollow center of the beam houses heating equipment; the beam itself serves as the supply and return plenum.

Bridge interior. *Nick Wood.*

The beam consists of plates welded into sections, which are bolted together. It supports the deck surface, the secondary structure, and all of the loads imposed on them. The beam also provides the necessary stiffness and allows other elements of the bridge to be replaced without threatening overall stability.

Aluminum was used for the bridge because of its light weight, strength, and low maintenance. The complete structure was preassembled off-site before being craned into position (see sidebar "London Bridge Is Going Up," p. 132).

Fixing tabs on the frame of the bridge are bolted to the ballet school's steel structure. At the opera house end, a steel angle, bolted to the concrete wall, supports rods on which the bridge structure hangs. This was necessary to absorb movement. Insulated metal collars at either end of the bridge provide entry and mediate between bridge and structure. Louvers in The Royal Opera House collar provide intake and extract openings for ventilation.

A tongue-and-groove wood floor sits on battens atop the beam. It, too, narrows in the center—to a width of 1,100 millimeters. Electrical connections are threaded between the battens. The floor stops about 75 millimeters shy of the glazing, creating an open area for heated air supply and intake.

Each portal, assembled from aluminum flats and capped on the interior and exterior with aluminum and oak, rotates 4 degrees. The glazed sides—two clear and two translucent—perform a quarter turn along the length of the bridge, twisting and overlapping to conceal the floor and compensating for the misalignment of the thresholds at either end. (There is a 725-millimeter height difference in floor levels.) The glass is inset into the portals at differing angles, depending on where it is located. It is bonded to the aluminum with silicone. LED lights, located in the outside corners of each portal, illuminate the bridge in the evening.

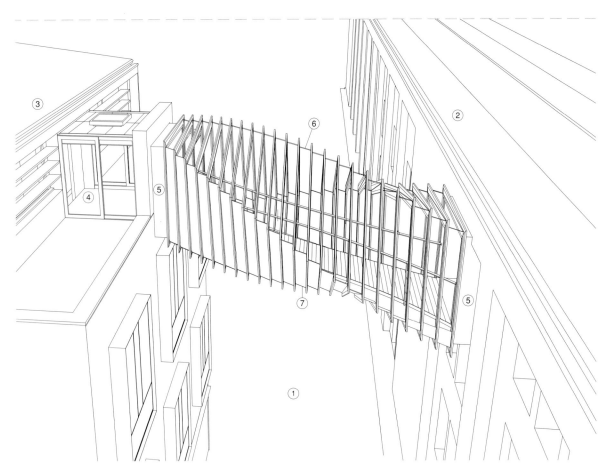

AERIAL PERSPECTIVE

1. FLORAL STREET
2. ROYAL OPERA HOUSE
3. ROYAL BALLET SCHOOL
4. BALLET SCHOOL VESTIBULE
5. ENTRY COLLAR
6. CLEAR GLASS
7. TRANSLUCENT GLASS

Connection to The Royal Opera House.
Nick Wood.

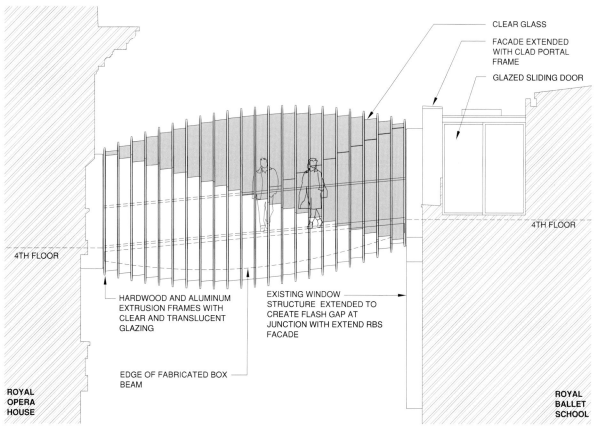

CLEAR GLASS

FACADE EXTENDED WITH CLAD PORTAL FRAME

GLAZED SLIDING DOOR

4TH FLOOR

4TH FLOOR

HARDWOOD AND ALUMINUM EXTRUSION FRAMES WITH CLEAR AND TRANSLUCENT GLAZING

EXISTING WINDOW STRUCTURE EXTENDED TO CREATE FLASH GAP AT JUNCTION WITH EXTEND RBS FACADE

EDGE OF FABRICATED BOX BEAM

ROYAL OPERA HOUSE

ROYAL BALLET SCHOOL

ELEVATION
The fourth-floor level of The Royal Ballet School is higher than the stage-plus-four level at The Royal Opera House. As a result, the ramp gradient is 1:12.

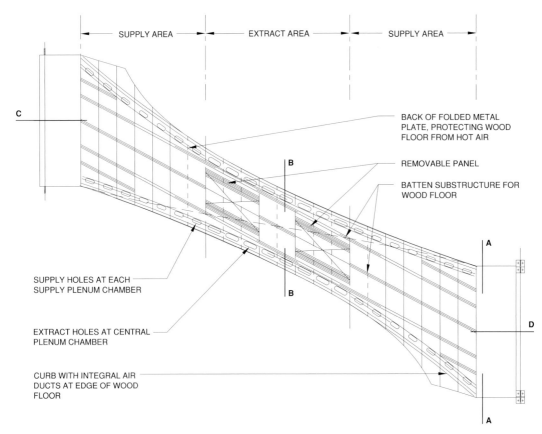

SUPPLY AREA — EXTRACT AREA — SUPPLY AREA

C

BACK OF FOLDED METAL
PLATE, PROTECTING WOOD
FLOOR FROM HOT AIR

B

REMOVABLE PANEL

BATTEN SUBSTRUCTURE FOR
WOOD FLOOR

A

SUPPLY HOLES AT EACH
SUPPLY PLENUM CHAMBER

B

D

EXTRACT HOLES AT CENTRAL
PLENUM CHAMBER

CURB WITH INTEGRAL AIR
DUCTS AT EDGE OF WOOD
FLOOR

A

PLAN DETAIL: FLOOR SYSTEM
Openings were left in the top plate of the beam for the fan coil heating units.

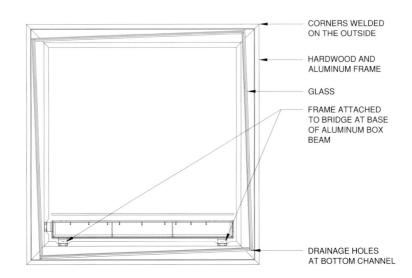

CORNERS WELDED
ON THE OUTSIDE

HARDWOOD AND
ALUMINUM FRAME

GLASS

FRAME ATTACHED
TO BRIDGE AT BASE
OF ALUMINUM BOX
BEAM

ELEVATION: FIRST FRAME
The frame is attached to the
bridge at the base of the
aluminum box beam.

DRAINAGE HOLES
AT BOTTOM CHANNEL

Wilkinson Eyre was asked to create an architectural element with a strong identity independent of the adjoining buildings. The resulting structure is primarily aluminum with wood trim pieces and glazed walls for light and views. *Nick Wood.*

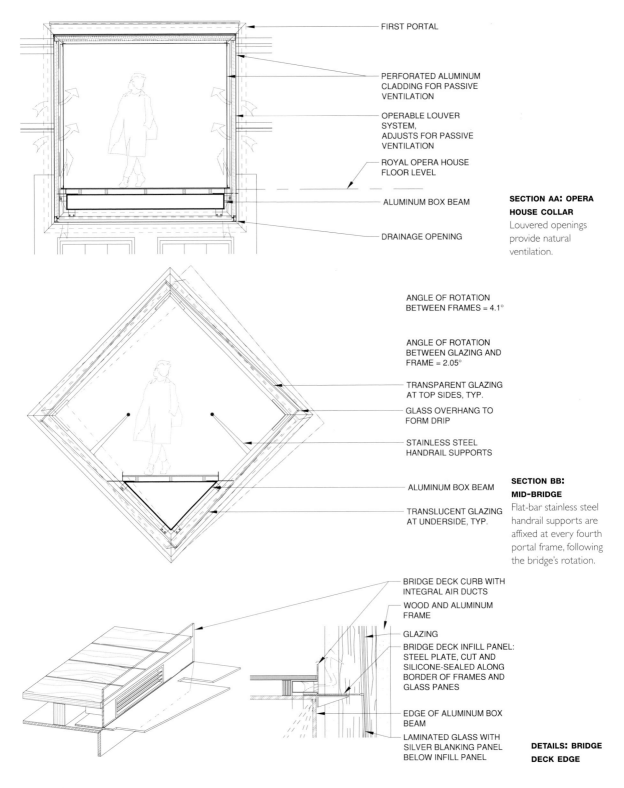

FIRST PORTAL

PERFORATED ALUMINUM
CLADDING FOR PASSIVE
VENTILATION

OPERABLE LOUVER
SYSTEM,
ADJUSTS FOR PASSIVE
VENTILATION

ROYAL OPERA HOUSE
FLOOR LEVEL

ALUMINUM BOX BEAM

DRAINAGE OPENING

**SECTION AA: OPERA
HOUSE COLLAR**
Louvered openings
provide natural
ventilation.

ANGLE OF ROTATION
BETWEEN FRAMES = 4.1°

ANGLE OF ROTATION
BETWEEN GLAZING AND
FRAME = 2.05°

TRANSPARENT GLAZING
AT TOP SIDES, TYP.

GLASS OVERHANG TO
FORM DRIP

STAINLESS STEEL
HANDRAIL SUPPORTS

ALUMINUM BOX BEAM

TRANSLUCENT GLAZING
AT UNDERSIDE, TYP.

**SECTION BB:
MID-BRIDGE**
Flat-bar stainless steel
handrail supports are
affixed at every fourth
portal frame, following
the bridge's rotation.

BRIDGE DECK CURB WITH
INTEGRAL AIR DUCTS

WOOD AND ALUMINUM
FRAME

GLAZING

BRIDGE DECK INFILL PANEL:
STEEL PLATE, CUT AND
SILICONE-SEALED ALONG
BORDER OF FRAMES AND
GLASS PANES

EDGE OF ALUMINUM BOX
BEAM

LAMINATED GLASS WITH
SILVER BLANKING PANEL
BELOW INFILL PANEL

**DETAILS: BRIDGE
DECK EDGE**

Aluminum and wood portal frames support the glazing. *Edmund Sumner/View.*

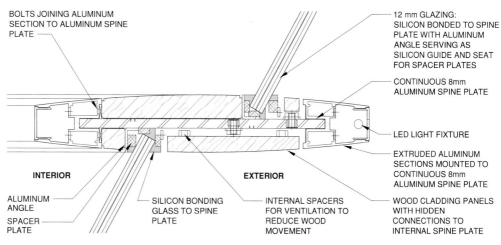

BOLTS JOINING ALUMINUM SECTION TO ALUMINUM SPINE PLATE

12 mm GLAZING: SILICON BONDED TO SPINE PLATE WITH ALUMINUM ANGLE SERVING AS SILICON GUIDE AND SEAT FOR SPACER PLATES

CONTINUOUS 8mm ALUMINUM SPINE PLATE

LED LIGHT FIXTURE

EXTRUDED ALUMINUM SECTIONS MOUNTED TO CONTINUOUS 8mm ALUMINUM SPINE PLATE

WOOD CLADDING PANELS WITH HIDDEN CONNECTIONS TO INTERNAL SPINE PLATE

INTERNAL SPACERS FOR VENTILATION TO REDUCE WOOD MOVEMENT

SILICON BONDING GLASS TO SPINE PLATE

ALUMINUM ANGLE

SPACER PLATE

INTERIOR

EXTERIOR

FRAME DETAIL

The 12-millimeter-thick tempered and laminated glazing is attached to the aluminum structure with silicone.

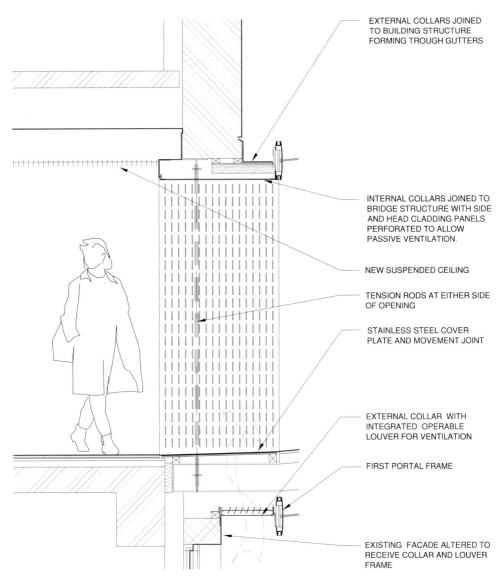

EXTERNAL COLLARS JOINED
TO BUILDING STRUCTURE
FORMING TROUGH GUTTERS

INTERNAL COLLARS JOINED TO
BRIDGE STRUCTURE WITH SIDE
AND HEAD CLADDING PANELS
PERFORATED TO ALLOW
PASSIVE VENTILATION.

NEW SUSPENDED CEILING

TENSION RODS AT EITHER SIDE
OF OPENING

STAINLESS STEEL COVER
PLATE AND MOVEMENT JOINT

EXTERNAL COLLAR WITH
INTEGRATED OPERABLE
LOUVER FOR VENTILATION

FIRST PORTAL FRAME

EXISTING FACADE ALTERED TO
RECEIVE COLLAR AND LOUVER
FRAME

SECTION C

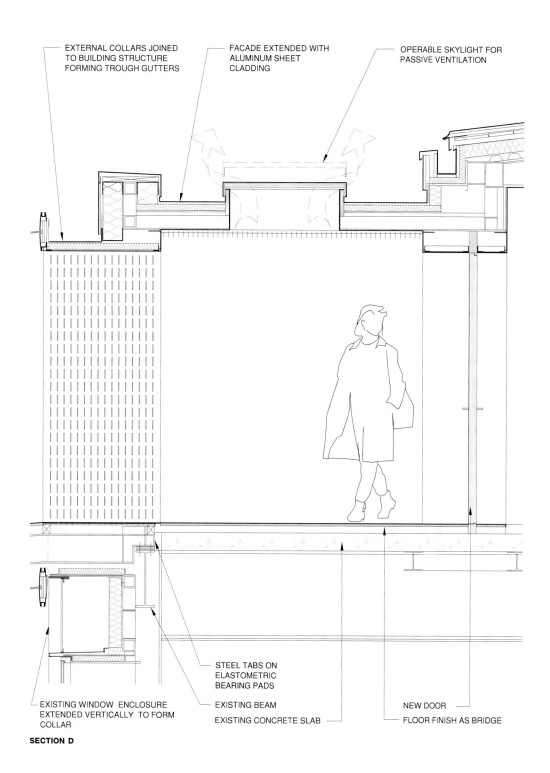

EXTERNAL COLLARS JOINED
TO BUILDING STRUCTURE
FORMING TROUGH GUTTERS

FACADE EXTENDED WITH
ALUMINUM SHEET
CLADDING

OPERABLE SKYLIGHT FOR
PASSIVE VENTILATION

STEEL TABS ON
ELASTOMETRIC
BEARING PADS

EXISTING WINDOW ENCLOSURE
EXTENDED VERTICALLY TO FORM
COLLAR

EXISTING BEAM

EXISTING CONCRETE SLAB

NEW DOOR

FLOOR FINISH AS BRIDGE

SECTION D

A) Off Site Construction

A1.) Beam Construction

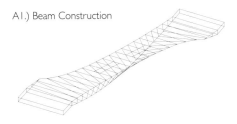

Beam design and construction included internal structural cross frames, welded aluminum web plates, frame cleats, and final end supports. Openings were left in the top plate for heating units.

London Bridge Is Going Up

Designing and building the Bridge of Aspiration required complex CAD geometry and handcrafting. The majority of the assembly was done off-site by Austrian-based cladding specialists GIG Fassadenbau.

A2.) Installation of cladding frames

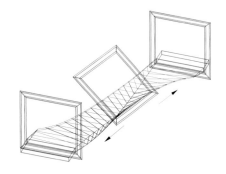

The frames or portals were also created and installed off-site. Work began at the center of the beam and proceeded to the supporting ends.

3.) Installation of glazing

Like the installation of the portals, the glazing was installed, starting at the center and working toward the ends.

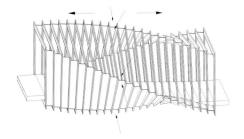

B) Work on site

B1.) Preparation work to
Royal Ballet School and
Royal Opera House

Reroute services,
demolition for opening,
strengthening work, making
good, installation of hanger
connections, erection of
scaffold across Floral Street
etc.

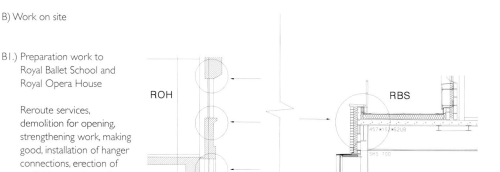

ROH

RBS

Meantime, at the site, the royal opera house and
the royal ballet school structures were prepared
to accept the fourth-story bridge—services
were rerouted, wall openings were created and
reinforced, hanger connections were installed,
and scaffolding was erected across floral street.

B2.) Bridge Installation

The entire assembly, 4.52 meters high and
3.92 meters wide, was carefully guided
through the streets of London on a four-
axle truck. The bridge was hoisted into
place by crane, and permanent connections
were made. Installation was completed in
less than two hours.

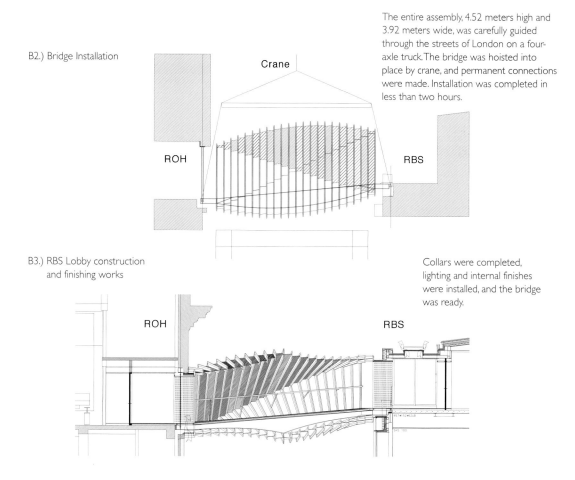

B3.) RBS Lobby construction
and finishing works

Collars were completed,
lighting and internal finishes
were installed, and the bridge
was ready.

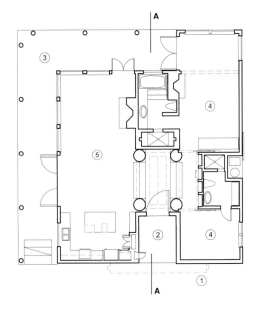

PLAN

1. LOG GUTTER
2. ENTRY PORCH
3. SIDE PORCH
4. BEDROOM
5. LIVING AREA

Pins Sur Mer, Mendocino County, California

Obie G. Bowman

A gutter carved from a redwood log creates an unmistakable entry.

Obie G. Bowman, AIA, wanted to celebrate the natural beauty of the redwood that grows so abundantly in Mendocino County, one of the leading producers of the unique timber. Rather than bury the wood inside the house, he discovered a way to say "redwood" right at the entry. The exaggerated gutter is a hefty chunk of debarked redwood trunk and, as Bowman says, "It keeps water from the roof from hitting you in the face when you walk into the house."

The 28-inch-diameter log sits on four sturdy brackets— also redwood. The brackets cradle the log, and the log is also notched to accept the brackets. Both elements, hand-shaped by the contractor, came from a nearby mill.

A broad V-cut in the top of the log is lined with galvanized steel. The metal tucks up beneath the edge of the galvanized steel roof, laps over the opposite edge of the V, and is hemmed at the tapered ends of the log.

A lag bolt recessed into the face of the V helps hold the log in place. At either end of the gutter, two $^5/_8$-inch threaded rods go through each of the brackets, the base of the log, and the 6-by-6-inch posts behind—part of the home's framing. Finally, steel strapping, anchored to the brackets and the framing, wraps each end of the log.

A 9½-foot-deep entry vestibule is located beneath the sharply sloped roof behind the log. The 5-by-10-foot painted steel door swings on five hinges for ease of operation. A 2-foot-square window sits in the middle of the door. Above, a clerestory window illuminates the vestibule with light from the house.

An approximately 20-foot-long, 28-inch-diameter redwood log gutter, as well as the brackets that help support it, were shaped by the building contractor. The vertical board siding on the house is also redwood. All these components came from a local lumber mill. *Tom Rider.*

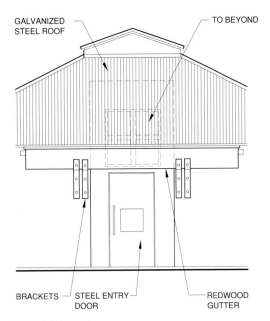

GALVANIZED
STEEL ROOF

TO BEYOND

BRACKETS   STEEL ENTRY
DOOR

REDWOOD
GUTTER

FRONT ELEVATION
The door handle is a standard stainless steel pull bar. The
lock is a conventional deadbolt.

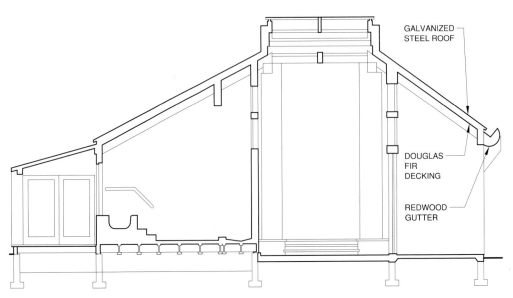

GALVANIZED
STEEL ROOF

DOUGLAS
FIR
DECKING

REDWOOD
GUTTER

SECTION AA
The deep vestibule precluded the need for a threshold; the limestone tile floors extend into the house. The ceiling
inside the entry is Douglas fir decking.

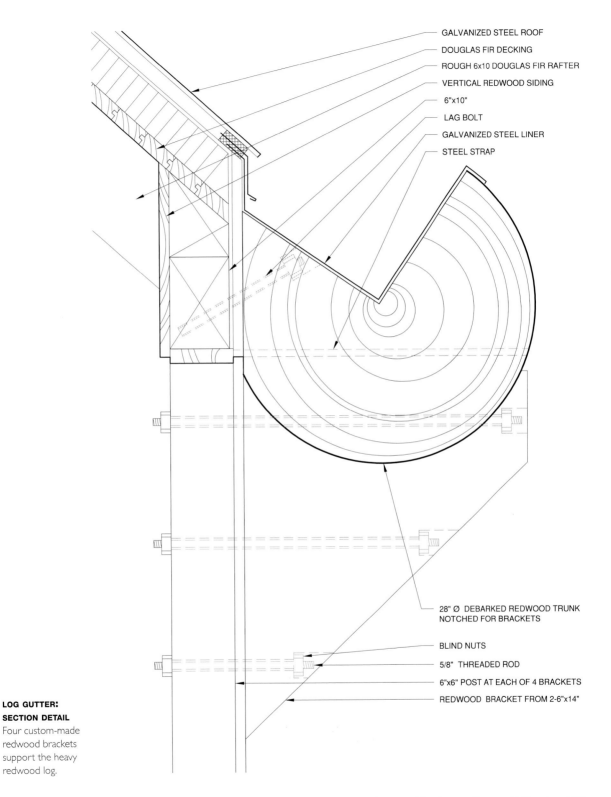

GALVANIZED STEEL ROOF

DOUGLAS FIR DECKING

ROUGH 6x10 DOUGLAS FIR RAFTER

VERTICAL REDWOOD SIDING

6"x10"

LAG BOLT

GALVANIZED STEEL LINER

STEEL STRAP

28" Ø DEBARKED REDWOOD TRUNK NOTCHED FOR BRACKETS

BLIND NUTS

5/8" THREADED ROD

6"x6" POST AT EACH OF 4 BRACKETS

REDWOOD BRACKET FROM 2-6"x14"

LOG GUTTER:
SECTION DETAIL
Four custom-made redwood brackets support the heavy redwood log.

Pins Sur Mer, Mendocino County, California   137

The Lucy House, Hale County, Alabama

Rural Studio Outreach

An interior wall of stacked plywood recalls the carpet tile exterior. *Rural Studio Outreach.*

PLAN

1. WINDOW BENCH
2. SMALL WINDOW
3. LIVING
4. BEDROOMS

Boxy, simple windows, built by students, adorn a unique energy-efficient house.

Rural Studio Outreach, a team of students assembled under the auspices of the School of Architecture at Auburn University by the late architect and teacher Samuel "Sambo" Mockbee, gives new meaning to the design/build process with their work on The Lucy House. Many of the details and even the structural system itself were developed in the studio and later refined in the field.

Originally conceived by Mockbee, The Lucy House is a collaboration of the Rural Studio and a national carpet manufacturer. This house was designed and built by seven Outreach students from around the world. It is the one of the last projects Mockbee directed before his death in December 2001; The Lucy House was finished eight months later under the direction of Rural Studio cofounder D. K. Ruth.

The walls are built of 72,000 carpet tiles stacked five at a time as "carpet bricks." These are held in compression by a heavy wooden continuous box beam. The wall system relies on the carpet for lateral stability. The weight of the roof is transferred to the foundation through structural metal columns embedded in the carpet wall. The wall also has a calculated R-value that is greater than 50.

A 21-foot-long window marks the front of the house. It consists of two large abutted sheets of ¼-inch tempered glass. These are set in a laminated plywood box. The box is almost 3 feet wide, sheltering the glass at the top and sides and providing a bench to sit on at the bottom. The box is divided in two places by the columns that are placed throughout the house. It is these columns that support the weight of the roof. The box beam that holds the carpet in compression runs along the top of the window. Below the bench is a standard framing system.

The interior plywood frames of the three small windows along the back of the house are flush with the walls. The exteriors project 4 inches from the outside wall, exaggerating their boxy shape. A 3-inch-wide steel angle wraps around the interior perimeter of each window to prevent racking.

The frames and the double-hung windows inside them are set in place on the carpet tiles and held secure by compression. The edges of the carpet are concealed with a plywood trim piece.

The carpet-walled section of the house is the family area. The crumpled tower, which sits atop the family's tornado shelter, is a bedroom for Anderson and Lucy Harris. The bottom of the front window frame is broad enough to be used as a bench. *Tim Hursley.*

STUDENTS' ORIGINAL CONCEPT DRAWING
The house is built of carpet tiles salvaged from office buildings throughout the United States. The selected tiles were older than seven years, minimizing off-gassing of volatile organic compounds.

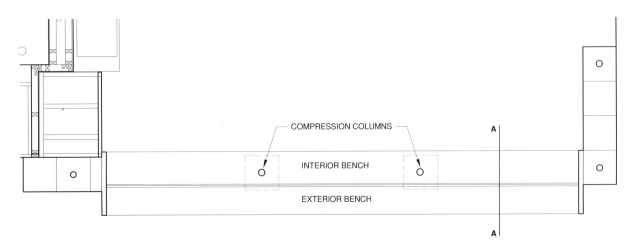

COMPRESSION COLUMNS

A

INTERIOR BENCH

EXTERIOR BENCH

A

FRONT WINDOW: PLAN DETAIL
The large front window was built with donated glass. The two pieces of glass float within a groove cut into the plywood.

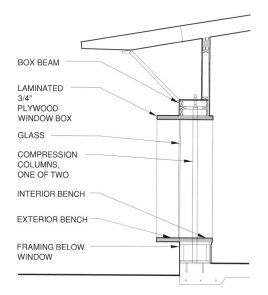

BOX BEAM

LAMINATED
3/4"
PLYWOOD
WINDOW BOX

GLASS

COMPRESSION
COLUMNS,
ONE OF TWO

INTERIOR BENCH

EXTERIOR BENCH

FRAMING BELOW
WINDOW

**SECTION AA: LARGE
WINDOW**
The windows are
protected from the
elements by the Rural
Studio's trademark
"big roof."

Tim Hursley.

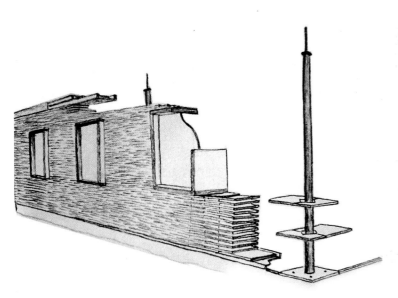

STUDENT'S STUDY: CARPET SYSTEM

Steel columns are located between the three back windows. These carry the roof load and are topped by a heavy wooden continuous box beam that holds the carpet in place. This building system is typical of the organic process used on The Lucy House and many of Rural Studio's projects, where a nascent idea is refined in the field based on the materials that are donated or what the students find.

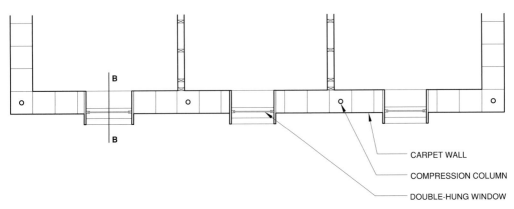

CARPET WALL

COMPRESSION COLUMN

DOUBLE-HUNG WINDOW

BACK WINDOWS: PLAN DETAIL

Stacking the carpet tiles during construction. *Rural Studio Outreach.*

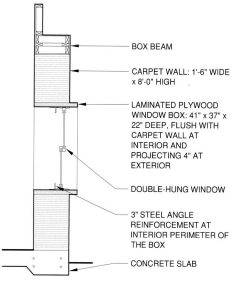

BOX BEAM

CARPET WALL: 1'-6" WIDE x 8'-0" HIGH

LAMINATED PLYWOOD WINDOW BOX: 41" x 37" x 22" DEEP, FLUSH WITH CARPET WALL AT INTERIOR AND PROJECTING 4" AT EXTERIOR

DOUBLE-HUNG WINDOW

3" STEEL ANGLE REINFORCEMENT AT INTERIOR PERIMETER OF THE BOX

CONCRETE SLAB

SECTION BB

The three back windows are held in place by compressing the surrounding carpet tiles between the box beam and the slab. The double-hung windows were installed after the continuous box beam was secured. A plywood trim piece covers the rough carpet edges.

The boxy window frames are 2-inch laminated plywood. The double-hung windows were donated to the project. *Tim Hursley.*

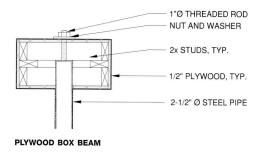

1"Ø THREADED ROD
NUT AND WASHER

2x STUDS, TYP.

1/2" PLYWOOD, TYP.

2-1/2" Ø STEEL PIPE

PLYWOOD BOX BEAM

The Lucy House, Hale County, Alabama   143

CREDITS

Hilltop Studio, Pasadena, California
Architect: Marmol Radziner and Associates, Los Angeles;
    Ron Radziner, design principal, Scott Walter, project
    manager, Chris Lawson, project architect, Scott Enge,
    in-house fabricator
Completion: November 2002
Size: 1,200 square feet
Materials used: Hot-rolled steel, glass, maple floors and
    ceilings, tatami mats, cedar soaking tub and bath
    finishes, polymer concrete sealer topping, concrete
    countertops
General contractor: Marmol Radziner and Associates
Mechanized sliding screens: Don Le Force Associates, Inc.,
    Rancho Dominguez, California
Linear metal stock: Dan's Custom Metal, Commerce,
    California
Glazing: Geisler's Glass, Chatsworth, California
Doors and windows: Marmol Radziner and Associates
Photos: Benny Chan

Pier 11/Wall Street Ferry Terminal, New York City
Architect: Smith-Miller + Hawkinson Architects, Laurie
    Hawkinson, principal in charge; Alexis Kraft, project
    architect; Christian Lynch, Nam-ho Park, Starling Keene,
    Ellen Martin, Karin Taylor, Todd Rouhe, Anne Hindley,
    design team
Size: 3,872 square feet

Completion: 1999
General contractor: Frederic R. Harris, New York City
Engineers: Ove Arup & Partners, New York City;
    Mahadev Raman, principal (structural; M/E; fire
    safety, sanitary)
Lighting design: Claude Engle and Associates, Washington,
    D.C.
Landscape architect: Judith Heintz Landscape Architecture,
    New York City
Materials: galvanized sheet steel, corrugated metal, exposed
    structural steel, aluminum curtain wall, terne-coated
    stainless steel, glass and aluminum hangar door, plywood,
    stone
Photography: Paul Warchol, Erieta Attali

Chicken Point Cabin, Northern Idaho
Architect: Olson Sundberg Kundig Allen Architects, Seattle
Designers: Tom Kundig, FAIA, principal designer; Steven
    Rainville, AIA, Debbie Kennedy, design team
Size: 3,400 square feet
Completion: 2003
General contractor: MC Construction, Spokane, Washington
Metal and glass contractor: All New Glass, Auburn,
    Washington
Engineers: Monte Clark Engineering, Columbus, Montana
    (structural); Keen Engineering, Seattle (mechanical
    performance spec.); Moser, Inc., Spokane, Washington

(design/build mechanical system); Phil Turner, Turner Exhibits, Lynwood, Washington (gizmo and mechanics designer)
Materials: 12-inch CMU, 1¼-inch ABX Marine Plywood, concrete floor, 3-by-12-inch exposed Douglas fir joists (lower roof framing)
Lighting: Pauluhn Electric Manufacturing
Locksets: Corbin Russwin
Custom hinges: McKinney
Closers: Dorma
Other specialty manufacturers: Steve Clark, Bellingham, Washington (custom casework); Fleetwood Windows & Doors, Corona, California (noncustom windows); Star Steel, Spokane, Washington (oversized door handle)
Photography: Mark Darley/Esto, Benjamin Benschneider

House Rua Suiça, São Paulo, Brazil
Architect: Isay Weinfeld Arquiteto, São Paulo, Brazil; Elena Scarabotolo, project manager; Ana Luisa Pinheiro, Carolina Maluhy, Isis Chaulon, design team
Associate architect: Arch. Domingos Pascali
Size: 7,664 square feet
Completion: September 2001
Construction: Epson Engenharia
Engineers: Aluisio Dávila (structural)
HVAC: Teknica Engenharia
Installations: Grau Engenharia
Materials: limestone floor, glass mosaics, stone, wood, steel, old brick, stucco, aluminum
Lighting: Companhia de Iluminação; Reka Iluminação
Flooring: Rocamat (limestone); Aroeira (old wood flooring)
Woodwork: Aroeira (wooden interior panels); Legno & Cia (closets)
Window frames: Metalúrgica Tambelini (aluminum)
Photography: Romulo Fialdini

Modular VII Chiller Plant, University of Pennsylvania, Philadelphia
Architect: Leers Weinzapfel Associates, Boston; Jane Weinzapfel, AIA, principal in charge; Andrea Leers, AIA, consulting principal; Joe Raia, AIA, project manager; Cathy Lassen, project architect; John Kim, Mee Lee, Anne Snelling Lee, AIA, Tom Chung, AIA, Ellen Altman, AIA, Jim Vogel, AIA, project team
University of Pennsylvania: Omar Blaik, vice president of facility management; Titus Hewryk, university architect; Juan Suarez, university engineer; Brenda Loewen, project manager; Dave Bryan, director athletic facilities/operations; Bob Seddon, head baseball coach
Client representative: Trammell Crow Co.
Engineer: William J. Trefz Consulting Engineers Inc. (M/E);

Keast and Hood Co. (structural); Boles, Smyth Associates, Inc. (site/civil); Richard Mabry P.E. (geotechnical)
Construction manager: Sordoni Skanska USA
Landscape architect: Michael Van Valkenburgh Associates
Lighting designer: LAM Partners
Photos: Peter Aaron/Esto

Maurice Villency Flagship Store, New York City
Architect: Thanhauser Esterson Kapell Architects, New York City; project designers: Charles Thanhauser, AIA, Jack Esterson, AIA, Andrew Ojamaa, Sheldon Catarino, Alejandro Sarasti, Derek Cote, Cordula Roser, Dirk Zschunke
Size: 30,000 square feet
Completion: October 2002
General contractor: Bauhaus Construction Corp., New York City
Metal and glass contractor: Landmark Architectural Metal and Glass, Brooklyn, New York
Engineers: Trevor Salmon, New York City (structural); Lilker Associates, New York City (M/E/P)
Lighting design: Earleylight, Providence, Rhode Island
Materials: Aluminum, stainless steel, glass (clear, sandblasted, and laminated starfire), West African Avodire wood, Bluestone, aluminum composite material (Alucobond)
Glazing: PPG Starphire fabricated by Floral Glass, Hauppauge, New York
Framing system: Efco Corp., Monett, Missouri
Lighting: Lightolier, Falls River, Massachusetts
Aluminum composite canopy: Alcan Alucobond, St. Louis
Hardware: D-Line, Denmark
Locksets: Schlage
Hinges, closers: Dorma
Photography: Brian Rose

The Reuters Building @ 3 Times Square
Architect: Fox & Fowle Architects, New York City
Size: 855,000 rentable square feet
Completion: 2001
General contractor: Tishman Construction Corp, New York City
Engineers: Severud Associates, New York City (structural); Jaros Baum & Bolles, New York City (MEP)
Curtain wall consultant: Heitman Associates, Chesterfield, Missouri
Curtain wall contractor: Glassalum International Corp., Miami; Diamond Installations, New Rochelle, New York; W&W (Pilkington Wall), Nanuet, New York
Photography: David Sundberg/Esto; Fox & Fowle Architects

West End House Boys and Girls Club, Inc.
Executive director: Andrea Howard
Architect: Leers Weinzapfel Associates; Josiah Stevenson, principal in charge; Ellen Altman, AIA, project architect; Dominic Passeri, Kelle Brooks, Tian Tian Xu, design team
Size: 31,000 square feet
Completion: March 2002
General contractor: Beacon Skanska
Metal and glass contractor: Tower Glass
Engineers: LeMessurier Consultants (structural); Cosentini (M/E/P)
Lighting design: Leers Weinzapfel Associates
Materials: Ground face CMU, aluminum and glass façade, steel structure, precast concrete planks
Glazing: Viracon
Lighting: Encompass
Door manufacturer: Efco
Locksets: Schlage
Closers: LCN
Photography: Anton Grassl

The Collins Gallery, West Hollywood, California
Architect: Patrick Tighe Architecture; Patrick Tighe, AIA, principal, Jeff Buck, Mike Yee, Jason Yeager, David Orkand, Rene Tribble, Joe Dangaran, design team
Size: 1,400 square feet
Completion: July 2002
General contractor: Tso Construction, Venice, California
Engineers: Joseph Perazzelli, Los Angeles (structural)
Materials: Stainless steel tube frame pivot door, zinc cladding panels, wood (framing), precast concrete steps, aluminum-frame curtain wall
Metal fabricator, doors, hardware: Tom Farrage & Co., Culver City, California
Glazing: Metal Window Corp.
Cladding: Rheinzink
Lighting: Lightolier
Hinges, closers: Rixson
Sunscreen, privacy shade: Mechoshade
Photography: Art Gray

National Civil Rights Museum Expansion Tunnel Entrance Gate, Memphis
Exhibit Planning and Design: Ralph Appelbaum Associates, New York City; Ralph Appelbaum, principal; Marianne Schuit, project director; Chip Jeffries, project designer; Ulrick Desert, senior designer; Todd Palmer, interpretive planner; Atsede Elegba, content coordinator; Ricardo Mulero, Dominique Ng, Amy Stoltz-Chase, designers;

Nadia Coen, senior graphic designer; Matteo Bologna, Vivi Hsin-Yi Hsu, graphic designers
Size: 12,800 square feet (expansion only)
Completion: September 2002
Architectural renovation: Looney Ricks Kiss, Memphis
Lighting: Technical Artistry
Materials: Powder-coated steel gate
Exhibit Fabricator: 1220 Exhibits, Nashville
Gate Fabricator: Herndon & Merry, Nashville
Photography: Albert Vecerka/Esto

12 Sutton Row, Westminster, London
Architect: John McAslan + Partners, London; Hiro Aso, Umberto Emoli, James Macauley, John McAslan, Michael Pepper, Anne Wagner, design team
Size: 26,000 square feet (net)
Completion: September 2002
General contractor: Interior, London
Project manager: Buro 4, London
Engineers: Price & Myers, London (structural); BDSP Partnership, London (M/E/P)
Quantity surveyor: Capita, London
Lighting design: John McAslan + Partners with Equation Lighting Design, London
Photography: Peter Cook, James Macauley

Scorpion Residence, Scottsdale, Arizona
Architect: Jones Studio, Inc., Phoenix; Eddie Jones, AIA, principal, Neal Jones, AIA, president
Size: 4,600 square feet
Completion: 2001
Contractor: Construction Zone; Andy Byrnes, principal in charge; Michael Groves, Project manager; Rod Svoma, master carpenter
Cast-in-place concrete: Construction Zone; Ron Congdon, field supervisor
Titanium cladding: Metalworks; Doug Vance
Millwork, swimming pool: Construction Zone; Rob Rubin
Granite/limestone: Imperial Tile; Alex Cohen
Furniture consultant: Jim Bartels
Landscape architect/contractor: Tonnesen Inc.; Bill Tonnesen
Engineers: JT Engineering; Jack Trummer (structural); Roy Otterbain Engineering (mechanical)
Mechanical contractor: Wolfgang's Cooling & Heating; Tim Graves
Lighting designer: Akali, Miho Schoetiker
Electrical contractor: Ferguson Electric, Bill Ferguson
Plumbing contractor: Ayoub Plumbing, Robert Johnson
Custom metal work: KG Custom, Kevin Gipson
Photography: James McGoon, Mark Boisclair Photography

Trenton Central Fire Headquarters and Museum
Architect: Venturi, Scott Brown and Associates, Inc., with The Vaughn Collaborative, associate architect; and M.K.N. Associates; Robert Venturi, Daniel McCoubrey, designers
Size: 54,000 square feet
Completion: 2002
General contractor: Roland Aristone
Metal contractor: Capitol Steel
Glass contractor: J.E. Berkowitz, LP
Engineers: Harrison & Hamnett, P.C.(structural); Marvin Waxman Consulting Engineers (mechanical); Donald F. Nardy and Associates, Inc. (E/P); Trenton Engineering Co., Inc. (civil)
Lighting design: Arclight
Materials: brick, steel frame, glass curtain wall, steel lettering
Glazing: PPG Industries
Lighting: McPhilben, Lincar Lighting Corp., Matalux, Halo, Paramount, Canlet, Pauluhn Electric Manufacturing, Lithonia
Door manufacturer: Raynor; Chase Industries
Hardware: Construction Hardware Inc., Warminster, Pennsylvania
Locksets: Schlage
Hinges: Hager Companies
Closers: Rixson
Photography: Matt Wargo for Venturi, Scott Brown and Associates, Inc.

Mii amo Spa at Enchantment Resort, Sedona, Arizona
Architect: Gluckman Mayner Architects; Richard Gluckman, FAIA, Dana Tang, Gregory Yang, project architects; Marwan Al-Sayed, Mark Fiedler, Carolyn Foug, Alex Hurst, Antonio Palladino, Nina Seirafi, Michael Sheridan, Julie Torres-Moskovitz, Dean Young, project team
Size: Spa building 24,000 square feet; casitas 10,000 square feet
Completion: January 2001
General contractor: Linthicum Constructors
Engineers: Rudow & Berry, Inc., Scottsdale, Arizona (structural); Clark Engineers SW, Inc., Phoenix (M/E/P); Shephard-Wesnitzer, Inc., Sedona, Arizona (civil)
Landscape architect: Ten Eyck Landscape Architects, Phoenix
Photography: Harry Zernike

The Brasserie, Seagram Building, New York City
Architect: Diller Scofidio + Renfro; Elizabeth Diller, Ricardo Scofidio, principals; Charles Renfro, project leader; Deane Simpson
Size: 7,000 square feet

Completion: January 2000
General contractor: Construction by Design
Metals: Carroll Todd Studio; Sanchez/Nitzberg
Glass: Creative Glass, Depp Glass
Woodwork: Superior Architectural
Upholstery: Hudson Valley Auto Interiors
Resin: Atta Inc
Custom plasterwork: Fresco
Media: Sharff Weisberg
Custom lighting fixtures: David Weeks
Engineers: Alan Burden, Structured Environment (structural)
Video collaborator: Ben Rubin, Ear Studio
Lighting design: Richard Shaver
Script for entry installation: Douglas Cooper
Curtain design: Mary Bright
Graphics: 2X4
Artwork casting: Z Corporation
Outcast installation assisted by Matthew Johnson
Photography: Michael Moran

Johnson-Jones Residence, Phoenix
Architect: Jones Studio, Inc., Eddie Jones, AIA, designer
Size: 4,500 square feet
Landscape architect: Bill Tonnesen, Tempe, Arizona
Engineer: J.T. Engineering, Inc., Phoenix (structural); Bruce Kolinski, Phoenix (civil); Otterbein Engineering, Phoenix (mechanical)
General contractor: The Construction Zone, Ltd., Rich Fairbourn, Andy Byrnes, Burt Little, superintendent
Lighting design: Lighting Dynamics, Phoenix
Concrete: Progressive Concrete Works, Phoenix
Rammed earth: Rammed Earth Development, Tucson
Steel structure: HI-TECH Fabrication & Erection, Phoenix
Miscellaneous steel: Thermofabrication, Mesa, Arizona; Metal Products, Phoenix; KG Custom Metal Works, Phoenix; Mandall Armor Design & Mfg. Inc., Phoenix
Millwork: Stradlings Cabinets & Millwork, Mesa, Arizona; Hank Loynd; Ken & Todd Laurent, Phoenix
Hardware: Clyde Hardware Co., Phoenix
Glazing: Glassline, Jim & Connie Knight, Glendale, Arizona; Diamond Glass & Mirror, Scottsdale, Arizona
Doors: Aztec Door Manufacturing Co., Phoenix
Metal cladding: Jeff Koenig, Cave Creek, Arizona
Drywall/painting: MKB Construction, Inc., Phoenix
Granite: Imperial Tile Imports, Phoenix
Pool: Showcase, Inc., Phoenix
Pond: American Fiberglass, Phoenix
Electrical: Ferguson Electric, Cave Creek, Arizona
Mechanical: Wolfgang's Cooling & Heating Corp., Phoenix

Audio-video: Electronic Design Group, Scottsdale, Arizona

Lighting: Creative Designs in Lighting, Phoenix; Lightolier Arizona, Phoenix; Light Up Your Life, Phoenix

Security: Mesa Security Systems, Mesa, Arizona

Photography: Timothy Hursley

Entrance canopy for Marriott East, New York City

Architect: Perkins Eastman Architects, New York City, Nicholas Leahy, AIA, principal, project architect; Roland Baer, AIA, principal, project manager; Jonathan Stark, AIA, principal-in-charge.

Advanced Structures Inc., Marina Del Rey, California, Robert Garlipp, project designer; Prakash R. Desai, engineer of record; Franz K. Safford, principal in charge

Size: 700 square feet.

Completion: August 2000

Constructor manager: Bovis Lend Lease, New York City

Canopy fabricator and installer: Advanced Structures Inc., Marina Del Rey, California

Canopy structural engineer: Advanced Structures Inc.

Building structural engineer: Goldstein Associates PLLC, New York City

Lighting design: H.M. Brandston & Partners Inc.

Glazing: W&W Glass, Nanuet, New York

Materials: Custom fabricated painted steel, glass

Photography: Chuck Choi Architectural Photography

Corning Museum of Glass, Corning, New York

Architect: Smith-Miller + Hawkinson Architects, New York City; Henry Smith-Miller, principal in charge; Ingalill Wahlroos, project architect; John Conaty, Flavio Stigliano, Ferda Kolatan, Oliver Lang, May Kooreman, Eric VanDer Sluys, Mauricio Salazar, Christian Lynch, Alexis Kraft, Ellen Martin, Paul Davis, Maria Ibanez de Sendadiano, with Jennifer Beningfield, Kevin Cannon, Wanda Dye, Anne Hindley, Robert Holton, Joern Truemper, Irina Verona, design team

Size: 117,400 square feet

Completion: 1999

General contractor: Louis P. Ciminelli Construction, Rochester, New York

Engineers: Ove Arup & Partners, New York (structural, M/E, fire safety, sanitary); Mahadev Raman, principal

Lighting design: Claude Engle and Associates, Washington, D.C.; John Wood, principal

Landscape architecture: Quennell Rothschild and Partners, New York City

Materials: large-format, low-iron polished plate glass; tempered and laminated glass; custom-designed, high-strength stainless steel structural systems; exposed structural steel; architectural concrete; anodized aluminum; stone; plywood

Photography: Paul Warchol, Judith Turner

The Royal Ballet School "Bridge of Aspiration," London

Architect: Wilkinson Eyre Architects, London; Martin Knight, project architect; Jim Eyre, director in charge; Annette von Hagen, James Marks, team.

Completion: March 2003

Size: 9.5-meter span

Engineers: Flint & Neill Partnership, London (structural); Buro Happold, London (environmental)

General contractor: Benson Limited, London

Lighting: Speirs and Major Associates, London

Bridge subcontractor: GIG Fassadenbau GmbH, Attnang-Puchheim, Austria

Photography: Nick Wood; View Pictures, Edmund Sumner

Pins Sur Mer, Mendocino County, California

Architect: Obie G. Bowman, AIA, Healdsburg, California

Size: 1,400 square feet

Completion: 1998

General contractor: Helmut Emke, Custom Builders, Gualala, California

Metal and glass contractor: Prieto Sheet Metal, Jenner, California

Engineers: Steve Pestell, Structural Engineer, Windsor, California (structural)

Materials: redwood, painted metal roofing, gypsum wall board, limestone

Glazing: Cardinal, Minnetonka, Minnesota

Lighting: Stonco, Barrington, New Jersey; Abolite, Cincinnati

Door manufacturer: Steelcraft, Cincinnati

Hardware: Trimco, Los Angeles

Locksets: Schlage

Hinges: McKinney, Scranton, Pennsylvania

Photography: Tom Rider

The Lucy House, Mason's Bend, Hale County, Alabama

Architect: Rural Studio; 2001-2002 Outreach Studio project, Auburn University School of Architecture, Auburn, Alabama; Ben Cannard, Philip Crosscup, Floris Keverling Buisman, Kerry Larkin, Tate, Marie Richard, Keith Zawistowski, student design team; Samuel Mockbee, D.K. Ruth, Andrew Freear, Johnny Parker, Jay Sanders. faculty; Melissa Foster Denney, Ann Langford, Brenda Wilkerson, Rural Studio office

Local collaborators: Hale County Department of Human Resources

Funding: Interface Carpet, Jesse Ball duPont Fund, Graham Foundation, Potrero Neuvo Fund

Size: 1,300 square feet.

Completion: Summer 2002

Materials: Carpet tiles, plywood, steel, concrete

Carpet tiles: Interface Carpet, Scotch Plywood, Hydro Stop

Glazing: Pella Windows and Doors, Druid Glass of Tuscaloosa

Framing system: Gamble Steel, Alabama Bolt and Supply

Lighting: Tuscaloosa Electric

Door manufacturer: Pella Windows and Doors

Other specialty manufacturers: Real Goods, Dowdle Gas

Material donations: Interface Carpet, Gamble Steel, Alabama Bolt and Supply, Scotch Plywood, Pella Windows and Doors, Druid Glass of Tuscaloosa, Hydro Stop, Anti Hydro, Tuscaloosa Electric, Real Goods, Dowdle Gas

Expertise donors: Robert McGlohn (structural), Fred Fulton (septic), Mike Thomas (contractor), Al Burson (dome enthusiast), Charles Jay (contractor), James Stegall (contractor)

Photography: Timothy Hursley; The Lucy House: Rural Studio Outreach

INDEX